Acknowledgments

I would like to thank my professors for their inspiration throughout my studies and career, and my husband, Mr. Istvan Zuh, for his support.

Psychology Life Hacks

Rebecca Zuh

This book is intended to inform readers about psychological well-being and is not a substitute for professional medical advice, diagnosis, or treatment. It is important to consult a physician for health-related concerns, particularly with respect to any symptoms that may require diagnosis or medical attention, and before making changes to health regimens. The content is provided 'as is' without any warranties, and results may vary based on individual circumstances. The author is no longer a registered psychologist; the material is drawn from past professional experience and is shared for general informational purposes only.

Realized Way Publishing

Adelaide, SA

First Edition - ISBN: 978-1-7641503-0-9

Improve your everyday level of happiness

by using the strategies in this book

~ ~ ~

Contents

Preface

This book presents practical psychological strategies to enhance your everyday happiness. Drawing from my extensive background, including three degrees in psychology, spiritual and personal development courses, and personal experiences, I have compiled the most impactful teachings and philosophies I know. Over the years, I have experimented with numerous belief systems. This book distills the most effective strategies I have used personally and professionally to boost and sustain psychological health.

The strategies are presented in an easy-to-apply manner, with guidance on how to incorporate them into your daily life. Each short chapter is tailored to address specific areas, providing a practical resource for enhancing your psychological health. By using this book, you will be more equipped to make positive changes and be prepared for challenges that may arise.

Introduction

With nineteen years of experience as a clinical psychologist, I have developed this book to share practical strategies based on cognitive behavioral therapy (CBT), enriched by the spiritual and philosophical teachings and courses I have studied. These methods, which can be effective for those facing psychological challenges, are presented in an approachable manner, drawing from both professional practice and personal experience.

Throughout my career, I observed that individuals who naturally resist depression often use simple techniques, sometimes unknowingly, to maintain happiness and manage stress. This book brings those strategies, which I have seen benefit countless clients, into your everyday life to enhance your psychological well-being.

The power of storytelling has been impactful in my practice. As a way to convey complex concepts through relatable anecdotes, this book includes such stories, anonymized to protect confidentiality, and used to illustrate effective psychological strategies.

Whether you seek relief from depression or anxiety or simply wish to increase your overall sense of wellbeing, each chapter offers stand-alone insights that may be read selectively, according to your needs. The book serves as a supportive resource, while also recognizing the essential role of professional help for severe psychological issues.

Although I am no longer a registered psychologist, this book is informed from my nineteen years of professional experience in clinical psychology, as well as my ongoing work as a life and wellness coach. Many of the strategies presented have been developed and refined over time, influenced by my professional background and continued personal study across psychological, spiritual, and philosophical domains.

References to "clients" throughout the book may reflect individuals I supported during my time as a psychologist, as well as those I have worked with more recently in a coaching capacity. Where real-life examples are shared, identifying details have been altered to protect privacy.

This book is intended to be an accessible resource and is not a replacement for therapy or medical treatment. For individuals experiencing significant mental health concerns, seeking appropriate professional support is strongly recommended. If you are facing significant emotional difficulties, psychological trauma, or are feeling unsafe, I encourage you to access assistance from a mental health service. For many other concerns, the strategies within these pages may offer valuable assistance.

Essential Tips to Reduce Depression: How to Feel Happy

Release yourself from your "old story"

During the first session of therapy, clients will often communicate to me a summary of their "life story." This can be a very beneficial way to release old stories that they have been holding on to. It also usually allows: 1) the client to gain another perspective on events from his or her past, and 2) the client can describe his/her life story knowing that he or she will not be judged. There may be particular stories that repeat in a client's mind from the past, and when the person has the opportunity to explain these in full, without being judged, it can be a very effective way to release him or her from these stories.

If clients try to tell or describe these stories to friends or family members, these people will usually interrupt and try and make the clients feel better about the past, suggesting that perhaps something did not occur in the way they remember it. The events may not have happened exactly as clients remember them; the important point is that they are able to express how they do recall the incident in full detail. People also may not know how to deal with narratives that involve someone feeling hurt or upset unless they have had specific training in how to deal with this. Therefore, if you feel you have never had the opportunity to voice your story, it may be a beneficial exercise for you to handwrite or type your story out as you perceive it in full. This will allow any old stories you are holding onto and any old hurt linked to them to be released.

Your story needs to not be written from a negative or victim perspective. It is far more useful to write the story from an observer perspective and in the third person. When you do this, you could also explore what else was occurring or may have been occurring at the time. This allows you to gain a wiser and broader perspective on the events of the past, which will help you to release them naturally.

What you decide to do with your story after writing it is entirely your choice. If your story is filled with hurt and pain, it might be best to write it once and then let go by destroying the material. In my experience working with clients, many have brought their completed stories to share with me during sessions. Sometimes, clients opt to publish their stories as books about their lives, using name changes to preserve anonymity. While this is an option, it is not necessary.

The true power lies in the act of releasing your story, which can lead to profound changes in how you view yourself and your past. I have personally used this method and found it to be highly therapeutic.

How your morning routine can impact your mood for the day

During the initial session with a client, I emphasize the importance of maintaining a morning routine. Often, when people are depressed, they hesitate to get out of bed, lingering with negative thoughts that only worsen their mood. I encourage clients to rise at a consistent time and maintain a morning routine to the best of their ability. A beneficial morning routine might include:

1. Set an alarm for 8:00 a.m. and aim to be ready by 9:00 a.m.

2. Prepare as if leaving the house, even if staying in, following the usual routines like showering, dressing, having breakfast, and grooming — such as shaving for men and applying makeup for women.

3. I also recommend to clients that they listen to their favorite uplifting music as they get ready.

A morning routine offers several benefits:

1. Achieving the tasks set within the routine boosts self-esteem.

2. It distracts from unhelpful thoughts and challenges, particularly important for those feeling depressed.

3. Consuming food and drinks at breakfast stimulates brain function.

4. Wearing 'nicer' clothes intended for going out can enhance mood.

A benefit of focusing on a morning routine is that it distracts a person from their potentially negative thoughts. This is especially important if people are tired, and I have noticed through my work, early mornings and late evenings are often a time when depressive thinking can peak.

With the morning routine, I therefore recommend clients remind themselves when they first awaken to delay analyzing how they feel until the time they have chosen to be ready by. Frequently people forget to check how they feel at this dedicated time, and this works well to elevate mood. I also encourage clients to accept with no judgment, they will likely feel a little negative with their thoughts as they have just woken up. These are tricks I will use myself to adjust my mood. Try it for yourself and see how it can work.

Completing a morning routine also sends a positive message about self-worth, motivating individuals to accomplish more, subsequently improving their mood. In my experience, clients who rise early and get ready tend to feel better throughout the day. Lingering in bed can exacerbate depression. The morning mood often sets the tone for the day, however, can be adjusted with various techniques.

While attending talks and workshops globally, I have noticed that many successful individuals share a common practice: a dedicated morning routine. They credit these routines for their sustained momentum and success. I have also found immense benefit in this practice, having adjusted my routine similarly.

If faced with a morning slump and tempted to stay in bed, try the above routine. In psychology, the principle of "opposite action" encourages doing the opposite of an initial reluctance — in this case, getting out of bed even when you don't feel like it — which can change both behavior and mood. If you are having a particularly difficult morning, take it one step at a time. Start with something as simple as sitting up in bed, then putting your feet on the floor, standing up, and setting a first goal, such as making yourself a cup of tea. Proceed to the next step and so on. Sometimes, when people are very depressed, incremental small steps are needed to get moving.

A morning routine significantly influences how one feels throughout the day. Identify morning behaviors that help you feel your best and ensure you allocate time for these activities. For example, a walk or jog in nature might rejuvenate and help focus on the day ahead. A previous prime minister in South Australia emphasized morning walking as crucial for his focus. Others might prefer journaling or relaxing in their garden. Make sure to allow time for breakfast and other morning activities, such as reading the paper.

I have learned from talks in India that even the Dalai Lama, known as one of the happiest people on the planet, begins his day needing a moment to uplift his spirits. He disclosed that he often wakes up in a 'bad mood' until he has his morning tea and spends time reading. His routine illustrates how fundamental morning rituals can be for mental well-being.

Prioritizing a routine that suits you is essential for mental health. Note how you feel when investing morning time for yourself versus when you don't. Spending thirty minutes to an hour in the morning is not time wasted. It energizes you, potentially leading to greater productivity and enjoyment throughout the day. Mornings can be crucial for establishing your mood for the day.

Physical factors to address

The majority of clients I have worked with come to me with a diagnosis of depression. When we discuss their objectives in therapy, they usually say they want to "feel happy." During the initial session, I work with clients to address the physical factors that may be affecting their mental health. Examples of factors that may be affecting their psychological health include tiredness, physical pain/illness, hormonal factors, alcohol withdrawal, vitamin/nutrient deficiency, dehydration, and hunger. I explain to clients that these are the main physical factors that may be impacting their emotional state.

I also explain to clients that if they are affected by one or more of the factors mentioned above, it is important to address these physical aspects to assist them in reducing depression. For example, if they feel tired, it can help to have a quick sleep; if they are hormonal, they may need to take a supplement; if they are in pain, they may need to take medication for pain relief. I recommend that clients discuss their physical health with their doctor if required.

Due to the impact that physical health can have on a person's emotional health, I spend time encouraging clients to increase their self-care in all areas. I ensure they are eating a regular and balanced diet, drinking plenty of water, receiving adequate sleep, and managing pain levels effectively. Often when clients are depressed, areas of self-care become neglected, and this usually exacerbates the depression.

I also explain to clients the need to take regular exercise as this is an important component in reducing depression (Blumenthal et al., 2007). When people exercise, endorphins are released into the body which can improve mental health (Dishman & O'Connor, 2009). If clients can exercise regularly outdoors, they will also be exposed to sunlight, which facilitates the body's production of vitamin D — a vitamin that has been found to assist with mental health (Stewart et al., 2014).

If you notice that you are feeling "down," it is always a good idea to check on the physical factors that may be affecting your mental health. If you are affected by one or more physical factors as described above, address these issues first, and your mood is likely to improve. The more you can care for yourself physically, including taking regular exercise, the less likely you will be to suffer from depression.

Distraction Techniques

"Distraction techniques" are strategies that encourage clients to focus on completing tasks to distract them from their thoughts as discussed in the 'morning routine' section.

After completing tasks and taking a "break from thinking," people usually feel better. When people are depressed, they tend to do less and shy away from activities they would normally enjoy. During therapy, I encourage clients to set small tasks for themselves to complete throughout the day; accomplishing these tasks often helps reduce depression. A task could be something small, like doing the laundry or tidying a drawer. It can help if individuals say to themselves, "I am not going to think about anything right now. I am just going to complete this task, then I will see how I feel."

Engaging in physical activities stimulates "feel-good" chemicals in the body. Furthermore, clients will feel pleased with themselves for accomplishing the task they set themselves to achieve. I usually encourage clients to attempt tasks they would normally complete regularly if they were feeling better. When people are depressed, they will often forget what they used to regularly enjoy doing. Gradually returning to these activities helps reduce depression levels.

It is important to start with small, achievable tasks early in the day, such as making the bed. When clients begin to feel better, we gradually increase the number of tasks and activities they set themselves. As they complete more, their energy levels increase, enabling them to achieve more and start to feel better.

This strategy can be effective for those feeling depressed or "down." The next time you feel this way, try completing a small task and observe the difference it makes. The motivation section contains additional strategies to help you begin tasks even when you might not feel like it.

A distraction technique does not always have to be a task you physically complete. It could also include activities like reading a book or watching a comedy movie. A distraction technique is essentially a strategy to divert your attention from thoughts of depression, which can, in turn, help reduce the feeling of being depressed. You can combine a physical task with listening to music or playing a comedy movie in the background. This can be a powerful way to distract yourself and change your mood.

The power of music to change your mood and reduce depression

A powerful strategy to change a client's mood is to listen to uplifting music. Research has demonstrated the effectiveness of music in alleviating depression (Moasheri et al., 2016). With this strategy, it is important that the client listens to music which makes them feel good to change their mood to a more positive one. Music can have the opposite effect if it triggers sad memories or if the songs are particularly slow. I recommend that clients who are feeling "down" listen to the music they would usually enjoy when in a good mood, and leave this playing in the background.

I explain that initially, the music may feel uncomfortable to listen to as it will feel like a different vibration to the mood the clients are currently experiencing. However, if clients leave the music playing, their mood will gradually lift to match the music.

People usually choose music to listen to that matches the feeling they are experiencing; with this strategy, I encourage clients to do the opposite to assist them to change their mood. I recommend they always have their favorite music readily available to assist them improve their mood.

The next time you are feeling down, try experimenting by playing your favorite uplifting music and observe how quickly your mood can change.

How Your Mental Health Is Affected by Your Thoughts

Learn how to think like a happy person

There are certain ways of thinking that benefit people and help improve their mental health. Individuals who are happier and less prone to depression typically think in these ways; it is natural and normal for them to do so since this is what they are accustomed to doing.

There are many reasons why people adopt a variety of thinking styles that they carry into adulthood. Usually, people have learned to think in a certain way through their home and school environments. During therapy, I spend considerable time with clients addressing their thinking styles and encouraging changes where necessary to assist them to adopt ways of thinking that better serve their well-being.

What is cognitive behavioral therapy (CBT) and how to make this work for you

To assist a client to overcome depression, it is vital to address their thinking. This involves using CBT, or cognitive behavioral therapy strategies. It can be useful to understand the basics of CBT and adopt some of the principles as this can reduce current depression and decrease the likelihood of experiencing depression in the future.

Cognitions are thoughts, and thoughts affect emotions and mental health. Numerous strategies can assist clients develop healthier ways of thinking, thereby improving their mental health. I will cover several CBT techniques in this chapter.

The behavioral aspect of CBT refers to the impact of behavior and how it affects a person's thoughts, emotions, and mental health. Thoughts impact emotions and behavior, and this forms a triangular paradigm. I typically explain this and diagram a triangle to assist clients to understand the connection between their thoughts, behavior, and emotions.

In the therapy of CBT, thoughts and behaviors, and their interrelationship, are addressed; clients are encouraged to make changes where required to improve their mental health. There are also specific exercises I use with clients during therapy to demonstrate how to change their thinking or to illustrate where their thinking may be "faulty."

The goal of therapy is to facilitate a change in the client's thinking to develop a more balanced thinking style. CBT can assist in creating rapid changes in a client's mental health and is an essential component of the therapeutic process.

How your perception may impact your mental health

It is not what happens in life that disturbs people, it is their perception of events. This theory was advocated by Dr. Albert Ellis who was an important contributor to the development of CBT.

How people perceive an event directly affects how they feel. A story I explain in therapy to highlight this involves two scenarios. I encourage the clients to consider how different they would feel depending on what they think in each scenario. For example, I ask clients to imagine they are in bed one evening, alone in their house and hear a vase smash on the floor downstairs. In the first scenario, I explain to clients that if they believe the wind or a cat knocked the vase over, they would probably feel little and perhaps be annoyed that the vase had been broken.

However, in the second scenario, I ask how they would feel if they believed an intruder had knocked the vase over rather than the wind or a cat. In this second scenario, the feeling the clients would have will be completely different, and it would be normal if, in this instance, they felt afraid. The event itself has not changed — which is a vase smashing on the floor. The difference in how a person will feel will depend on their interpretation of the event.

This process occurs all the time in daily life, and clients often do not understand how powerful their perception of events can be in affecting their mental health. I explain that it is essential to be aware of their initial interpretation of events and then to adjust their thinking and consider alternative explanations. If they do this in a positive way, it can significantly improve their mental health.

For example, I have worked with clients who became depressed after losing their job. In this example, the event is "losing their job," and how the clients interpret the reasons for this will directly affect their mental health.

I have observed several cases where clients were fired, and they believed this was because they were, "incompetent at the work." Clients often use self-blame, for example, thinking that if they had not been consistently late, they might still have the job. However, I encourage them to view the situation from another perceptive. I have recommended to these clients to consider whether perhaps they lost their job for other reasons, such as there was not enough work, or the employer wanted to hire a relative.

I encourage clients to consider other factors that may have been occurring that they were not informed about. Rather than taking situations personally, I encourage clients to explore what else may have been happening behind the scenes. By considering these alternatives, clients are less likely to take situations personally, typically leading to an improved self-view and reduced depression.

To assist clients in re-framing their interpretation of an event, I encourage them to examine the evidence behind their thoughts. Returning to the job loss example, the client may have been employed for years without issues. Therefore, it would not be accurate for the client to assume they were not competent at the job. If this had been the case, it would have been an issue previously. If tardiness was problematic, it would likely have been addressed. Additionally, the employer may not disclose terminating one person to employ a relative due to legal concerns.

Another example I have observed in therapy is when a relationship ends suddenly. The event, in this case, is the "relationship breakup," and how the client perceives and interprets the event will affect their mental health. Clients may blame themselves for a relationship ending, believing their partner separated from them for a personal reason, such as because they were "lazy" or "depressed."

In these circumstances, the "evidence" a person may have used to draw a conclusion about a situation could be based on what someone said. In this example, the person leaving the relationship may have called the client these names. The point I highlight to clients is that what they were told may not be the truth. For example, if someone leaves a relationship, it may be because that person met someone else and may not want to inform his or her partner of this.

I encourage clients to challenge the evidence behind statements, such as whether calling them "lazy" or "depressed" seems fair. For example, if a client had been called these names, I encourage them to reflect on how much they contributed to the relationship and supported their partner.

I would also encourage the client to consider whether ending a relationship because a person is "depressed" is the right thing to do, and if he or she would leave a person for this reason. Clients will usually acknowledge that they would not separate from their partner if they were depressed. I also usually explain to clients that many other factors for ending the relationship probably were not disclosed for a variety of reasons. When clients recognize other reasons that their relationship ended, they tend not to take it as personally and do not feel as depressed about the situation.

The easiest way to adopt this thinking style is to consider the broader picture and always ask yourself, "What else may be going on in this situation?" rather than jumping to conclusions and turning to self-blame. It is always beneficial to question, "What is the evidence?" The more you can explore alternate explanations, rather than taking matters personally, the better you will feel about yourself.

The Power of Rational Thinking

Are you thinking in ways that make you feel good about yourself?

Do you give yourself a "mental jury?"

One of the first things I explain to clients is the importance of thinking in a balanced and rational way. Often, clients say to me they have been trying to "think positively," although they have not succeeded. This perceived failure can make them feel worse, as they believe they have "failed" at "positive thinking." Typically, the clients I see have experienced recent challenges, difficulties, or significant trauma. Simply instructing them to "think positively" is not helpful. Instead, I encourage them to acknowledge these challenges and help them to recognize how these challenges have made them feel.

The first important step is to acknowledge the events matter-of-factly. During therapy, I encourage clients to think more rationally about the events and acknowledge what has occurred or is currently happening. Clients are then guided to consider how things may be different in the future and to realize their potential for other opportunities.

I have worked with several individuals where, encouraging rational thinking significantly improved their mental health. For example, many people I have consulted with were not in relationships during treatment and believed they would, "never be in a relationship." This irrational thought increased their depression. In therapy, I encouraged these individuals to change their self-talk to be more realistic. They learned to adopt more rational thoughts, such as, "Although I am not in a relationship now, I could be in a pleasant relationship in the future." As clients adopted this different, more rational way of thinking, they began to feel better.

This method of adopting more balanced and realistic thoughts can be applied to any irrational thought you may have. The first step is to become aware of your thinking. We all have an internal dialogue that continually runs through our mind. It is important to notice whether this dialogue contains rational and logical thoughts or if there are irrational thoughts that need to be addressed.

By recognizing the thoughts running through your mind, challenging those that are irrational, and replacing them with more rational thinking, you can feel better about yourself and your circumstances. If you find you have an irrational thought about something, I recommend questioning:

- Is that a statement based on fact?

- Where is the evidence for and against this belief?

- Are you being fair to yourself?

- What would your friends say to you about that belief?

I find it helps to give yourself a "mental jury" to challenge the thoughts you may be holding and consider the evidence for and against a statement.

You can identify irrational thoughts through the language you use. Keywords to assist in identifying these thoughts are extreme words such as "never" and "always." Circumstances are not usually as extreme as this, and using more balanced language is more realistic. In psychological terms, when people use terms such as "never" and "always," it is referred to as "global" or "all-or-nothing" thinking. Situations are rarely "black" or "white." Encouraging people to explore the "gray" areas and consider alternatives increases thought flexibility, which can improve mental health.

It can be challenging to become aware of all the thoughts running through your mind and be able to quickly change them to balanced and logical thoughts. Be kind to yourself as you develop this new way of thinking. Changing thought patterns takes time. If you prefer, you can write a thought down to challenge it. This can be an effective way to gain a balanced and rational perspective.

I always advise people to "be interested" in their thoughts and not to be harsh on themselves, as some thought patterns may have been established for years. However, once you learn to use rational thinking more frequently, you will begin to develop a healthier way of thinking. Gradually over time, this will become your new way of thinking.

The benefit of not taking things personally

Are you only seeing the "tip of the iceberg?"

How understanding this can help you

This method of inquiry is useful in everyday situations with people. Individuals who are psychologically healthy often employ this technique. An individual's internal dialogue regarding a situation with a person directly affects how they feel about it. Here is an example I use with clients to explain this concept. I ask them to imagine they are walking down the street and see someone they know on the other side of the road, and they say "Hello." However, the person does not respond. I explain that the client will feel differently about this scenario depending on their interpretation of what occurs after they say, "Hello."

If the clients believe that their friend ignored them and perhaps is not speaking to them at the moment, they may feel upset. However, if they consider that the other person simply did not hear them, they will not feel any emotion connected to the event. Their initial thought might have been that the friend ignored them, however, thinking further, they consider another option — that their friend did not hear them.

Another scenario I describe involves a client who believes a work colleague may be upset with them. The colleague usually appears "happy" and talks to the client regularly, although on one day seems unwilling to speak. I explain to the client that instead of personalizing the situation and assuming the colleague is upset with them, it is more useful to consider what else might be affecting the colleague's mood that day.

I explain to clients that their initial perception is like seeing the "tip of the iceberg" and emphasize that we only ever see the surface of someone else's life experience. To assist clients in understanding this, I encourage them to consider factors in their lives currently affecting them. I ask if they are aware of all the details behind the scenes regarding the person or situation impacting them. For example, a person may be tired, in pain, or dealing with various scenarios outside of work, such as caring for a sick relative or moving house.

On any given day, people are affected by a variety of factors, and these factors are rarely known to others. Developing the habit of always considering what else might be occurring can assist your mental health rather than taking situations personally. Adopting this practice of secondary inquiry and not personalizing situations is likely to improve your mental health.

Avoid assuming anything: What are the facts?

How to address this and improve your relationships

I explain to clients that it is best not to "assume" anything. I describe how the word assume can be broken down into "ass-u-me," symbolizing the potential to make an "ass" out of "you" and "me." When they assume something, they form a belief or idea without having all the facts. In therapy, I have seen many examples where assumptions are inaccurate and, depending on the circumstances, can negatively impact relationships and the client's mental health. Often, one person in a relationship has an interpretation of an event, while their partner sees it differently, leading to friction due to misunderstandings.

I have observed many cases where a partner acts with the best intentions, which are then misinterpreted by the other. For example, one client explained to me that they left towels on the bathroom floor to keep the tiles warm for their partner, only to be seen as "lazy" or "untidy." Although this person had the best intentions, the misinterpretation by the partner caused stress in the relationship.

Through exploration of each person's true intentions during therapy, insight is obtained. By gaining information, rather than "assuming," individuals can address issues and improve their relationships. I have observed many cases where couples argue due to misunderstandings and assumptions, however, once clarified, improvements in the relationship usually occur.

It is beneficial to question situations and ensure you have accurate information and understand a person's true intentions rather than jumping to conclusions. It may be good to consider if you have been assuming in interactions with anyone, to discuss the issue further to clarify matters. This can usually shed light on a situation and improve the relationship or situation.

The Power of Language

Are there words you use every day that have an adverse effect on your mood?

What are the keywords to notice and remove from your vocabulary?

How using the word "should" can negatively affect your mental health: How to change this

The main words I see clients use that adversely affect their mental health are "should," "must," "ought," and "have to." During therapy sessions, I work through a handout with clients concerning these words and explain the potential impact on their mental health. When clients use these words, they place unnecessary pressure on themselves, which can lead to feelings of guilt or anger.

Frequently, when these phrases and thoughts are examined, people realize that the thought or idea originates from external sources, such as a well-meaning parent or societal expectations. When individuals recognize this and reflect more clearly on what they genuinely want to do instead of fulfilling external expectations, they typically feel better about themselves and their situations. This applies to both significant life decisions and smaller, day-to-day issues.

For example, societal expectations often presume that people will complete their education, marry, have children, buy their own home, and work in full-time employment. People may tell themselves they "should," "must," or "ought to" follow these expected life stages, which places pressure on them. I explain to clients that it is important they make choices aligned with their desires, independent of societal expectations. Releasing this pressure usually improves a client's mental health. I describe using the word "should" as "should-ing" on themselves, which adds unnecessary stress.

People might use this word for smaller, everyday matters without realizing it, such as saying they "should clean the house" or "should go to the shop." In these instances, it is helpful to consider whether these tasks are necessary immediately or can be postponed. Typically, many "should" statements are not urgent and may not need to be completed at all. I explain to clients that it will help them feel better psychologically if they replace the words "should," "must," and "ought" with phrases like "want to," "choose to," or "would like to." This shift highlights a preference rather than a pressure to perform tasks.

I also advise clients to notice if they use these words in reference to others. I recommend avoiding "should," "must," or "ought" regarding themselves or others. This reduces the pressure they may have placed on themselves or others. Additionally, clients need to be aware if they are using these words negatively, such as saying they "should not" or "must not" do something, especially if it is something they genuinely want to do and it would make them feel good.

Furthermore, I advise clients to avoid telling others they "should not" or "must not" do something. By examining their language and avoiding these words, clients can reduce the psychological pressure they may place on themselves and others. This often improves their relationships by removing expectations from themselves and others.

If you notice yourself using the words "should," "must," or "ought," explore where that idea came from and consider whether it is something you truly want to do. It may be interesting to observe when you use these words and try replacing them with alternatives that convey your choice rather than obligation. Becoming aware of and adjusting your language ensures that your decisions are based on personal desires rather than societal expectations or the need to please others. This can reduce psychological pressure and improve mental health.

How the word "should" relates to the suppression of emotions

Do you accept all your emotions?

Clients often tell me they believe they "should" or "should not" feel a particular emotion in different situations. When clients say this to themselves, they attempt to suppress the genuine emotion experienced and replace it with an emotion they think they "should" be feeling. This suppression can increase depression and decrease self-esteem. For psychological health, it is essential that all emotions are allowed and accepted. The first emotion felt does not cause psychological stress; rather, it is the interpretation clients give to that feeling that negatively impacts their mental health.

An example I have observed several times in therapy involves clients caring for a family member with a prolonged illness who then passes away. The client may feel relief when the person they cared for, perhaps for several years, has died. They often feel guilty about this relief, believing they "should" feel sadness. I clarify that they need to accept feeling relieved, as it is a valid emotion. I also explain that they may be feeling relief for the deceased, as that person is no longer suffering.

Another frequent scenario is when clients know someone who has died and believe they "should" feel sad when they actually feel no sadness. I have seen examples where clients did not have a good relationship with the deceased, yet they believe sadness is expected. I reassure clients that however they feel is okay and to accept this. They might even feel pleased that the person is no longer around and feel guilty about experiencing this emotion. I encourage them to accept however they feel and not feel guilty about any feelings they may have. I encourage clients to accept the emotions they experience and explain that this is important for their mental health.

However, I also advise clients that disclosing their private emotions in these situations is not necessary. In the examples above, I explain that their relationship with the deceased was unique. Others may have experienced an entirely different relationship with the person who died and therefore experience different emotional reactions. I emphasize to clients the importance of accepting others' feelings as well. Expecting others to feel a certain way can negatively affect one's mental health. I describe to clients that, depending on their personal experiences, they might experience a range of emotions, all of which are valid and need to be accepted.

I have also seen instances in therapy where positive events occur, and clients think they "should" feel happy. Clients I work with are often facing challenging experiences and are suffering from depression, so events that might normally bring joy, like a child's success at school or a friend's new job, do not evoke happiness. I reassure them that however they feel is okay, even if they perceive the emotion as negative, such as jealousy.

Clients might feel no emotion at all about events that previously brought joy. I explain that whatever they feel is okay, even if it is "nothing," and to accept this feeling. I describe how emotional states usually pass quickly, and while they might feel differently about an event later, or not, that is also okay. I stress the importance of accepting any emotion experienced in the moment.

To ensure psychological health, one needs to accept all emotions. Notice if you use "should" or "should not" regarding an emotion. If you do, try accepting the emotion without judgment. While expressing emotions is typically recommended, it may be more beneficial to maintain privacy with your genuine feelings and not disclose them in certain situations. Other people may not understand and might suggest you "should" or "should not" feel a certain way, which will not assist you. Ideally, everyone would accept all emotional states without judgment. Although, this is unfortunately not always the case.

Other words to watch out for

Are you "awfulizing" or "catastrophizing?"

Is a situation really "awful?"

The language clients use to describe events and imagined outcomes often dissuades them from participating or undertaking activities. This, in turn, may reduce their confidence and negatively affect their self-esteem. There are extreme words that clients may use that impact their mental health. I spend time during therapy examining the language a client uses in their internal dialogue and with others. Clients who are depressed and who have low self-esteem usually "catastrophize" when imagining or discussing situations or potentials. This is a tendency to exaggerate outcomes and expect the worst.

Clients will often say that something would be "awful" or "disastrous" if it occurred, which is an exaggeration, as situations are usually not that bad. For example, many clients who suffer from anxiety have said to me, without realizing they used the word, that it would be awful if someone they did not know spoke to them at the shops. Through therapy, I help clients to realize that although they may feel anxious for a few moments, they will be okay, and the situation will not really be awful.

Clients often use exaggerated language about imagined future situations. This can reduce their likelihood of participating in these events and strengthen the exaggerated perception of what they believe would happen. For example, a client may believe that if he or she told a joke and nobody laughed, it would be awful. This belief may prevent him or her from ever wanting to tell jokes, leading them to avoid this behavior. In reality, events are not usually as negative as clients imagine. In this example, I would explain to the client that it would pass; it would not really be awful, and they would be okay.

I work with clients to replace catastrophizing language with more realistic language, as in the examples above. It may be interesting to notice if there are any unrealistic or exaggerated words you use when considering participating in behavior, and if this discourages you from doing this. If you notice that you use particular catastrophizing language, try to change the words to a more realistic language. This will increase the likelihood of you participating in these behaviors and increase your confidence. I recommend that you also become aware of when other people use this language with you, and not to let others discourage you from doing things you would like to do.

The importance of perspective

As a therapist, I assist clients to develop more realistic language and perceptions about an event, by guiding them toward a balanced view of the situation. For example, in the cases mentioned above, I might ask clients whether this event would matter in the perspective of their entire lifetime. Would an event occurring now still be significant in five years' time? Would anyone even remember the event in two years? When clients realize that they have exaggerated the importance of an event and gain a more balanced perspective, they become more inclined to participate in a behavior. This, in turn, assists them to gain confidence and improve their mental health.

I would recommend that when you imagine participating in a future event, you notice your thoughts regarding it. Always assess whether you are placing exaggerated importance on an event. If you can maintain a realistic perspective, you will be more likely to try something new and increase your confidence.

Another word to avoid in language and why: "But..."

There is one more word I recommend clients try to avoid, and that is the word "but." I educate clients about how people generally use this word and explain why it is advisable to try not to use it. I explain to clients that when they use "but" they may be resisting saying what they truly mean. It benefits a client's mental health to express their feelings openly rather than suppressing them. I often provide examples of how they might have been using but while expressing themselves. For instance, a client might want to share their feelings although they fear expressing their true emotions. They might say something such as, "I do not want to hurt your feelings, but..."

After a person says the word but they usually follow with how they truly feel. Another example is when a client says, "I do not want to complain, but..." I encourage clients to express themselves more directly without using the word but.

It is interesting to observe how people use this word in language. I explain to clients that when they say but, they reveal their true feelings after using the word. I further explain that the words spoken before but are not their true feelings and essentially become erased by the word but.

It could be insightful to notice if and when you use this word, and to try finding a replacement word. Avoiding this word is important to ensure you express yourself honestly, and doing so can enhance mental health.

Psychological Tricks Happy People Use:

Attribution theory

Learning to be kinder and fairer to oneself

In therapy, I spend time explaining how people tend to attribute others' successes to internal qualities, while attributing their own success to external factors. For example, if someone scores highly on an exam, they might attribute their success to being "lucky." Conversely, if someone else achieves a high score, they are more likely to attribute it to that person being knowledgeable or intelligent.

Through assisting clients to understand this phenomenon, I encourage them to view their successes just as they would view another person's success and to challenge any negative or unfair attributions, they might make about themselves. It is essential for clients to acknowledge their successes and give themselves credit for their achievements to enhance their psychological health. It is also important for clients to be fair to themselves and, if they do not achieve something, to consider other factors that may have influenced their outcomes instead of blaming themselves.

I recommend becoming aware of whether you attribute your successes to personal qualities. The next time you achieve something or are successful, observe whether you acknowledge your accomplishments or dismiss them. It enhances psychological health to give yourself full recognition for your achievements. Additionally, it is important to be fair to yourself if you do not achieve something, and to consider other factors that may have affected the outcome rather than blaming personal qualities.

Tricks to enable you to see things more positively

People are often hard on themselves, although there are various strategies that may be used to challenge and address this. One trick I encourage clients to practice is identifying three positive aspects or things they like about themselves every day. This could include being kind to animals, considerate of others' feelings, or an adventurous person. Ideally, it is recommended to write these down and try to identify three different aspects they like about themselves each day. If clients struggle with this, I suggest they ask friends and family what they consider to be the client's positive attributes.

To help clients develop a more positive mindset, I also encourage them to identify three different external factors they are grateful for each day. These factors need to relate to anything outside of themselves. I suggest clients write these down in the present tense, such as, "I am pleased it is a nice sunny day today," "I am thankful I have a nice house to live in," or "I am happy I have a wardrobe full of clothes to wear." By doing these exercises regularly, clients begin to notice more and more positives, rather than always focusing on negatives or issues of lack. This practice leads to increased mental health and a positive mindset.

This technique may also assist with relationships. For example, if a parent is having difficulty with a child's behavior, they may focus increasingly on the child's negative or "bad" behaviors. This focus can increase the cycle of negative behavior, and the parent may start forming a negative perspective of the child. It can help if the parent reminds themselves of three attributes they like about the child every day — for instance, the child is creative, determined, and has nice blue eyes. As with the strategies described above, if the parent can identify three different positive aspects daily, it will benefit the relationship. Depending on the situation, it may also be helpful to inform the child of these attributes or mention them to a partner.

You can incorporate these strategies into your daily routine. I find it especially beneficial to do this early in the morning, as it can help bias your mindset to be more positive throughout the day. Over time, you will start to notice more positives during your day, and it will become easier to recognize these things. You can use these strategies to generally assist in becoming more positive in your thinking, which in turn helps you feel better. These strategies can also be applied to any situation in your life where you may notice you are viewing things in a particularly negative light.

Assertiveness Tricks

The importance of valuing your own needs

Many of the clients I have worked with struggle to be assertive about their own needs. Depending on their situations, they have often been psychologically "programmed" to prioritize others' needs over their own. This conditioning negatively impacts their self-esteem. Through therapy, I educate clients about becoming assertive and standing up for their own needs.

I explain that prioritizing their needs does not make them selfish and that it is beneficial to focus on their individual needs, sometimes even putting them ahead of others. This issue frequently arises with mothers of young children who do everything for their child and neglect their own needs. I advise that allowing themselves time to rest leads to feeling rejuvenated, which means they are more energized when spending time with their child. Taking time to rest typically enhances the quality of parenting for the remaining time.

I explain to clients that they need to give to themselves first in order to effectively give to others. I illustrate this with the example of the emergency procedure on airplanes, which stipulates that people need to place their own oxygen mask on before assisting others. This highlights the importance of self-care before caring for others; if someone places the oxygen mask on their young child before putting in on themselves and then passes out, who will take the child off the airplane?

Changing perspective

To assist clients, recognize that they may be expecting too much of themselves or doing too much for others, I encourage them to use a "changing perspective" technique. I ask clients to imagine if a good friend were doing everything they are, what would they think or say to them about the situation? For example, in therapy, I have often observed mothers struggling to complete all the household chores while taking minimal time for themselves. These mothers are often exhausted, yet they persist in a daily routine with no time for personal rejuvenation, which can eventually lead to depression.

I ask these clients to consider all the tasks they complete on a typical day and then reflect on what they would say if their friend completed all these tasks, without taking time for self-care. By imagining their friend in this situation instead of themselves, clients often realize how much they demand of themselves and recognize it as unreasonable. I also inquire if clients believe their friend, in this hypothetical situation, would need to take regular breaks. By picturing someone else in their situation, clients can often see more clearly that they are expecting too much of themselves and recognize the need to allow themselves time to rest.

During therapy, the first step with clients is to help them change their beliefs and recognize that prioritizing their own needs over others is not selfish; it is essential for their mental health. Once clients adopt this mindset, they find it easier to be more assertive about their needs.

Assertiveness versus aggression

I often spend time explaining to clients the difference between assertiveness and aggression. I clarify that being assertive is not the same as being aggressive, and there is nothing negative about being assertive. I typically work through a handout with clients that explains that when they are assertive, they adopt a respectful, balanced position. I emphasize that being assertive does not mean bullying others into doing what they want or being disrespectful of others' needs. I explain that the client's needs are important, and so are the needs of others. Many clients I work with tend to prioritize others' needs over their own, and I encourage them to work toward achieving balance through the strategies outlined in the sections below.

The "broken record" technique

Once we have addressed the client's thinking around assertiveness, I describe different methods for being assertive. One technique I explain is the "broken record" technique, which is used when someone is trying to persuade a person to do something they do not want to do. In this strategy, I explain to clients that they need to repeatedly express that they do not want to comply with the request, using slightly different wording each time, until the person stops asking.

With this technique, I explain to the client that they need to acknowledge the request and then repeat their needs and decision until the other person accepts it. For example, if someone asks the client to attend a party and they do not want to go because they are tired, the client could initially say, "I am tired and would rather stay at home." If the person asks again or tries to persuade them further, the strategy involves conveying the same message in a slightly different way, such as, "Yes, it would be nice to go to the party. However, I cannot because I need to get up early in the morning."

If the person persists, I encourage the client to repeat a slight variation, such as, "I would have liked to go to the party, although I am quite exhausted after a busy day, so I need to rest tonight." The key is that the client does not waver in their decision to stay home and rest. If the client remains steadfast, the person will eventually stop asking. I also advise clients that it is more effective to avoid using the word "no" with this strategy, as it often upsets people.

With this technique, I also explain the importance of maintaining a neutral, calm, and firm tone. Often, when people become frustrated because others are not complying with their wishes, their voices may get louder. I advise clients that if this happens, it is crucial to maintain an even tone and avoid raising their voices to match the tone of the other person's voice.

It is also important to try to maintain a neutral expression. This can be challenging, as it is frustrating when people do not accept when you decline a request. People tend to mirror facial expressions, therefore maintaining a neutral expression will assist to keep the conversation calm. Conversely, if frustration shows on your face, it will likely be mirrored back. Interestingly, this can help in many conversations that have the potential for disagreement.

When people initially start standing up for themselves, others may be surprised and might not appreciate this change. If a client has previously been "complying" with every request and suddenly starts to decline, the person making the requests may become upset.

However, over time, those making requests will get used to the client's new pattern, and any initial frustration will usually subside. If a person regularly seeks assistance from someone, and that person eventually refuses to comply, the requester will usually find someone else to meet their needs.

I recommend noticing if you regularly agree to complete tasks you do not want to do. If this is the case, you might try the strategy outlined here. This method is effective for any request, whether it is attending a social function or doing an extra work task. The key is to remain consistent in your responses. If you waver and then agree to the task, it sends a message to the person that if they push, you will comply. This will be remembered, and they will continue to ask you in the future.

It may also be interesting to observe if you need to use this strategy more often with certain people. If someone continues to try and persuade you to go along with their plan, despite your clear expression that you are tired or prefer not to participate for another reason, are they respecting your needs and feelings? Also, consider whether you would "push" someone in the same way. If you notice this pattern with certain people, you may need to adjust your boundaries, as it is important to socialize with those who respect your feelings. This can increase your sense of self-worth and worthiness, which is vital for mental health.

Learning how to use appropriate assertive language

Depending on the situation, I educate clients regarding how to use assertive language. Many of the clients I have worked with have never asserted themselves before and need to learn what to say when situations arise. Clients can often identify specific situations in which they would like to become more assertive, such as with their employer at work or with a friend or family member. If the client and I can identify a particular situation during therapy, we work on phrases that could be used when required. It also helps the client to practice saying these phrases out loud in the therapy session.

Assertiveness is a skill like any other and needs to be learned. I encourage clients to practice being assertive before encountering a situation. This preparation will make it easier for them to know what to say when the situation arises. For example, I often encourage clients to practice what they would say in a work setting where they want to assert themselves, or in a situation involving a friend or partner.

During the session, we decide on phrases that may be appropriate to use such as, "I would like to help out with that project, although I have a busy schedule at the moment."

Repeating these phrases multiple times is beneficial, as it makes them easier to use when required. It assists to acknowledge the request and respond with a phrase to decline, such as, "Thanks for asking, although that's not really in my job description," or "That does look like a very interesting assignment. However, I am busy with another project at the moment."

Steps to becoming assertive with your own needs

When clients first attempt to become assertive, it can be challenging for them to reject something immediately when asked to do something. This is often difficult, particularly if they have developed a habit of always saying yes immediately to others without really considering their own needs. I spend time with clients explaining the different strategies that can be used to work toward this. I spend time with clients discussing various strategies that can be used to progress toward assertiveness.

For example, if clients find it difficult to reject social invitations, such as going to a party, one strategy is to tell the person they need to check their diary or talk to their partner and that they will get back to them. Alternatively, in a work situation, they could say to a colleague or employer that they need to check their schedule or other commitments and will get back to them. This approach gives clients the breathing space to decide whether they want to attend the party or complete the extra work, and to consider how they might respond to the person asking.

As clients become clearer about what is in their best interests and as they learn how to be assertive about their needs, this process becomes easier over time. Clients also learn the assertive language they feel most comfortable using and begin to use these phrases more quickly as needed.

It may be interesting to notice if you agree to undertake tasks or projects you would prefer not to, or whether you assert your needs and decline requests when necessary. You may assert yourself in some areas of your life and perhaps not in other areas. The key is to be honest about what you want to do and how you want to spend your time, rather than complying with requests out of obligation.

Tricks to Help You Clear Your Mind from Worries

"Worry time"— a trick to clear your mind of worries

A creative problem-solving technique

There is a psychological technique called "worry time" that I have observed to be an effective strategy for assisting clients to think more clearly and reduce stress levels. This technique is beneficial for clients suffering from anxiety, depression, or stress. It serves as a strategy for clearing one's mind of worries, and I believe it may be useful for everyone.

People who are psychologically healthy and manage stress well often use a variation of this method regularly — for example, during their walk to work. They use this time as a regular time slot to allow all their thoughts and worries to clear as they walk. This practice is very important to maintain psychological health. The basis of the worry time technique is derived from an information sheet developed by (www.cci.health.wa.gov.au).

If clients do not have a regular time to allow thoughts to clear, stress usually accumulates as important thoughts are pushed to the back of their mind.

I explain to clients that they may go through an entire day exposed to noise or some type of activity, making it difficult for them to think clearly about important issues affecting their life.

From the beginning of the day, people often have music or the television playing in the background, or some other distraction from their electronic devices. When driving, they usually have the radio or music playing. People are generally exposed to constant background noise, whether at home, work, or on the road, from electronic devices or conversations. This continuous exposure to external sound can prevent them from clearing their mind of thoughts that may be causing stress.

Distraction may be a beneficial short-term strategy if a person is overwhelmed by their thoughts; however, for the long term, an effective strategy is required to manage thoughts and thereby reduce stress. When clients regularly practice the technique of worry time, I observe a reduction in their stress levels and an improvement in their mental health. Worry time is a strategy that is carried out in a specific way, and I spend time during therapy explaining the exact method to clients.

I explain that they need to allocate a specific time for their worry time, for example, from 5:30 pm to 5:40 pm, Monday through Friday. The chosen time needs to be when they are not tired, as thinking can often be more negatively biased when a person is fatigued. I usually recommend making this a daily practice, with each session lasting only ten minutes. If they do not have time during the week, they can complete it once at the weekend for a longer duration if needed.

Once you learn how to carry out the worry time strategy effectively, you will find you can move through topics quickly and you may only need a few minutes for this practice.

This strategy works well when combined with a walk, if possible. I explain to clients that it is necessary to walk in an area that does not require them to focus on where they are stepping. A walk in a familiar environment with an even surface is ideal. It is also important to ensure there are no distractions, such as walking a dog that requires attention. Completing this technique in silence is essential. I recommend to clients that it is better to either not take their telephone or switch it off, and to have no music playing. A short, silent walk around their neighborhood is sufficient.

I advise clients, as they begin their walk, to allow themselves to focus on thoughts and issues they would usually avoid thinking about, such as challenging questions they may be facing. During their worry time, they need to allow themselves to think about all the important areas and decisions in their life. These often include areas people avoid thinking about because they are too challenging and, indeed, may have no immediate "answer." However, it is important to consider these matters and explore possibilities with a solution-focused approach.

I recommend that clients start with the present day and move their awareness through all areas of their life, exploring potentials. For example, they need to consider all possibilities and decision-making around housing, finances, relationships, employment, health, and family. Other topics to consider could include holidays or social events. There may also be more of a social interaction issue they are concerned about, such as a difficult conversation they need to have with someone. This is a perfect time to explore and perhaps even rehearse the conversation, imagining how you will manage it when it arises.

I explain to clients the importance of focusing on one topic at a time, moving their attention from the present day forward, and considering all options once only. I recommend beginning by thinking about planned activities for the day ahead, then the week, and then the coming months, such as social events or weekends away, before moving on to potentially more challenging topics such as housing. This method assists to ease one into the practice of focusing on the future.

A person may then consider the issue of housing. I recommend they begin by reflecting on their current living situation, then explore all options related to their housing and future to run through their mind. For instance, would they move next year? Where would they move to? Would they sell the house, or would they rent it out? I encourage them to consider all possible options regarding their housing, exploring future possibilities as far as they can. For example, if they did move somewhere else, where would that be? How long would they stay there?

I explain to clients that once they have fully explored everything, they can think of related to their housing situation, they can then move on to the next topic. It is important for clients to check in with themselves by thinking a phrase such as, "That covers everything about housing, now what about health?" As they progress through these topics, new ideas may arise. I advise that it can be useful to make notes during their worry time so they can remember these ideas.

They may note down, for example, "Call accountant about my mortgage," or "Check house prices in the new area." I recommend that they go through all the topics one by one in this way. Once they have covered all topics and options, they need to perform a "mental check" to observe if there are any other "worries" or areas they have not yet addressed. When clients are satisfied that they have considered everything they need to, they can mentally note that they have finished their worry time and that it is completed until tomorrow, or their next scheduled worry time.

During their worry time, it is important that people focus solely on future circumstances and refrain from dwelling on past events or decisions. A worry is typically a future issue or decision to be made, and it is most beneficial to focus exclusively on these during worry time. Therefore, I advise clients to be disciplined about where they allow their mind to focus. I explain that if they find their thoughts drifting to other topics, they need to redirect their attention back to the intended focus, such as decisions around housing.

It is also very important with this technique that clients address all worries once only, pushing decisions as far as they can within each area. People often contemplate difficult questions repeatedly throughout the day without reaching any conclusions. The tendency can be to avoid thinking about challenging subjects in depth, as doing so may feel overwhelming. However, it is far more effective to consider an issue just once, exploring it in as much detail as possible using a solution-focused approach.

I also explain to clients that this is their private decision-making time, and they do not need to share their ideas about their future with anyone. During their worry time, it may be necessary to consider difficult topics, such as whether to leave a partner or change employment. It is important for individuals to allow themselves private time to reflect on such issues if needed. I explain to clients that it may be more beneficial to make their own decisions about these matters rather than discuss them with others. It is also better for their psychological health to acknowledge these thoughts rather than trying not to think about difficult matters. When people attempt to suppress issues, it often results in mental pressure and stress.

The other essential component of the worry time technique that I describe to clients is the need to recognize when a worry enters their mind during the day. A worry will usually concern a future issue that needs to be addressed, such as, "How am I going to pay that bill?" or "Where could I move to?"

I explain that when clients identify a worry, they need to acknowledge it as a worry and tell themselves they will consider it during their worry time, mentally setting the thought aside until later. This approach is far more effective than trying to suppress the thought and push it to the back of their mind. I also recommend that, if clients prefer, they may write down these worries throughout the day and refer to the list when they carry out their worry time.

Once clients make worry time a regular habit, they usually find that their mind becomes clearer. Instead of thoughts being scattered throughout the day, they have an allocated time to address their worries, which generally makes them feel more relaxed. Often, the knowledge that their worries will be addressed later allows them to subside and occur less frequently. This enables a person to focus on other matters during the day.

I usually recommend that clients try this strategy for a week to see how different they feel. Once people begin practicing worry time, it often becomes a regular habit, enabling clearer thinking and a more relaxed state of mind. You may already have an allocated quiet time when you allow your mind to clear. However, thinking regularly in the structured manner described above can significantly increase your problem-solving efficiency. It is an interesting technique to try, and it usually helps people think more clearly. It trains a person to consider issues once in detail rather than repeatedly contemplating issues several times without reaching solutions.

This is a technique I practice regularly, and I find that if I become busy and forget to carry it out, I start to feel stressed. I notice that if I ignore issues or decisions that need attention, they seem to become louder in my mind, and my thoughts do not feel as clear during the day. As soon as I allow myself the time for worry time, I feel much more relaxed.

Challenging Beliefs Around the Past

Are you holding on to an experience from your past, and is this affecting your mental health?

How to overcome this

In therapy, I often observe that a person's depression is driven by a specific thought or phrase concerning a past event. People frequently blame themselves for something and hold onto a negatively biased story about what they believe they could have done differently. Clients often think that if they had done "X," then "Y," would have happened, and the circumstances would have been more favorable, or something could have been avoided. This belief is examined in therapy in an unbiased manner, and alternative scenarios are considered. The "old story" needs to be discussed in full to allow for its release.

During this technique, I encourage clients to focus carefully on the circumstances they were aware of when the past decision was made. People often forget that there were many factors they learned about later, and there would have been no way to know these factors at the time of the decision. Old guilt and blame are released when people accept this perspective. I explain that individuals make the best decision they can with the information available to them at that time. Often, clients have held onto a story for years, believing they did something "wrong," without examining it in a fair and logical manner.

I have worked with individuals exploring past stories they have held about a variety of scenarios. For example, I have observed several people who were convinced their adult children were traumatized because they had not separated from an aggressive partner earlier. These individuals believed that their children would have been perfectly fine had they left the aggressive person sooner, given that this person had been verbally and emotionally abusive toward them.

Through careful exploration of this belief and the circumstances at the time, these individuals were able to accept that they separated from the aggressive partner when they were able to. Furthermore, they were able to realize that leaving the person earlier might have resulted in more negative consequences for both themselves, and their children. When they recalled the threats of violence from the aggressive partner, they acknowledged that an earlier separation might have led to their partner pursuing them and causing physical harm.

These individuals also recalled that there were many circumstances affecting their decision to stay, which they had forgotten over time. For example, they might have had to live on the streets if they left earlier, with no money for food. This would have been dangerous and would certainly have impacted on the children's health.

Through exploring all potential options and scenarios and being realistic about their choices at the time, these individuals were able to accept that they did their best in the situation. Rather than believing that leaving earlier would have made things significantly better, they understood that the situation could have been worse.

These individuals were able to recognize that they were brave to leave their partners when they did and that they had managed to raise their children safely on their own. While there may be some level of trauma experienced by the adult children due to early exposure to abuse, the parent came to understand that the situation could have been much worse.

With this technique, it is important to explore possible negative consequences as well. For example, I have worked with several individuals who fought in wars and held guilt throughout their lives about shooting and killing someone. By thoroughly exploring these cases, they were able to understand that if they had not shot the enemy, it was highly probable they would have been killed themselves, and there were no alternatives at that time.

It is essential that no details are overlooked when exploring a past incident in this manner. If any details of the event are missed, the mind may fill these gaps with unrealistic scenarios, and guilt about the past event may not be fully released. For example, I have consulted with individuals who served in the army and believed they might have been able to injure people instead of killing them. However, upon close examination of their individual circumstances at that time, they had to accept that under attack, they reacted in defense and had no choice in that moment.

There have been additional layers of guilt with these clients, such as regret about joining the army. However, when examined thoroughly, these individuals were able to understand that there were no other employment options at the time and that they needed to work to support their families. I have often seen depression lift very quickly, as in the examples above, when people accept that they did their best given the circumstances, even if their best in that particular situation was to shoot someone.

The examples above are quite extreme and represent the types of scenarios that may present during therapy. However, even individuals who are psychologically healthy may carry stories about the past where they believe they could have done "better," leading to regret about decisions made. Generally, the fewer stories such as these, a person holds, the better they will feel psychologically and about their choices in life.

If you can identify an event from the past where you feel guilty or believe you made the "wrong" choice, you may wish to explore this belief in the manner I described above. This might concern a choice of partner, financial investment, where you chose to live, or employment decisions. If you identify an event where you feel you made the wrong choice, try to examine it once only, thoroughly, and in complete detail. It is crucial to explore all angles of the scenario, also considering that the outcome could have been worse if you had not made the decision you made at the time.

I recommend completing this exercise alone. However, it can be helpful to imagine what you would say to someone else who had experienced that event, and to consider any factors they might have overlooked that influenced their actions or decisions at the time. Strive to be realistic and fair in your appraisal of the past event. You will know when a new understanding or insight is reached because you will experience an "aha!" moment of realization.

If the thought ever enters your mind again, or if any other thoughts indicating you "could have done better" arise, remind yourself that you did the best you could at the time. If you can accept that you made the best decision with the information you had, this old story will be released, and you will feel better knowing you did your best.

This technique can also be applied to more minor day-to-day situations. The key to noticing when there is something to address, is that it will repeat in your mind, and you may question your actions, believing you could have done more or handled a situation differently.

This might be something such as worrying that you cut off another driver in traffic and they had to brake suddenly. When reflecting on the situation afterward, consider that your decision to pull out when you did may have helped avoid an accident. The other driver may not have been aware of traffic on the far side of your vehicle, although you were. It is helpful to remind yourself that you did the best you could in that moment.

If a thought about a situation repeats in my mind, I analyze it once, quickly and thoroughly, allowing it to be released. When you become accustomed to doing this as needed, it helps reduce stress by minimizing concerns over past actions you may be dwelling on.

Strategies to Reduce Anxiety: What Really Works?

What is "normal" anxiety?

As a therapist, one of the most common issues clients present with is anxiety, which can affect people in various ways. Clients may experience acute episodes of anxiety, often referred to as "panic attacks," where they fear they might "pass out," or they may suffer from social anxiety. Anxiety levels vary from client to client. However, there are several strategies that can assist clients, which I have described below.

Initially, I explain to clients that everyone experiences anxiety in certain situations. I describe to them the circumstances in which it is normal to feel anxious, such as when taking an exam. I also explain that most people would experience a low level of anxiety when completing a new task for the first time, such as on their first day at a new job. In a stressful situation like this, a degree of anxiety is actually beneficial, as blood and oxygen flow are increased during mild anxiety. This response helps a person concentrate and focus during these times, thereby enhancing performance.

I also explain to clients to be careful not to label all feelings of increased oxygen and blood flow as anxiety. People who have suffered from anxiety often tend to label all these sensations as anxiety, forgetting that there are other times they may experience heightened awareness in the body, such as when they feel excited.

During therapy, I discuss with clients the times they might feel excited and encourage them to recognize how this feeling could be wrongly labeled as anxiety. It is important for clients to begin perceiving that anxiety can be positive or useful and that they may even be experiencing a feeling of excitement.

Managing acute anxiety episodes

How your internal dialogue can increase or reduce your anxiety

To treat anxiety, I explore with clients their internal dialogue regarding anxiety, trying to discern what they say to themselves during their most anxious times. Often, people have health concerns about their heart or breathing related to their anxiety experience. Part of the therapy process involves examining these thoughts and the evidence supporting them. I explain that their internal dialogue can either exacerbate or alleviate their anxiety.

For example, one of the most common phrases clients tell themselves is that they may be "having a heart attack," which, in turn, increases their anxiety. I explain to clients that they need to challenge this thought and replace it with something such as, "It may feel like I am having a heart attack, although I am healthy and I have never had a problem with my heart. Therefore, it is most likely an episode of anxiety."

To challenge their thoughts during therapy, I usually ask clients how many times they believed they were having a heart attack and how many times they actually experienced one. Clients may not have considered that they have never truly had a heart attack. Realizing this often helps reduce their fear, as they come to understand they have not been thinking rationally about the situation.

I also emphasize that although they may have experienced many episodes of anxiety, which might have been uncomfortable, they have always survived these episodes. The more clients can apply and remind themselves of these balanced thoughts when they feel anxious, the more likely their anxiety levels will be reduced.

Depending on the circumstances, I often recommend that these clients undergo a professional health examination to check their heart function. This provides reassurance that their heart is healthy, making it easier to accept that there is nothing physically wrong. By reminding themselves of this during moments of heightened anxiety, they can often slow their heart rate and breathing, which, in turn, reduces the intensity of the anxiety.

The other main health concern I have observed in clients with anxiety relates to their breathing. Clients often worry that they may "stop breathing" or that their "throat will close." I explain that during anxiety, their breathing rate will increase, as it does for everyone.

I further emphasize that this is a normal and healthy mechanism of the body; understanding this helps reduce their fear around these sensations.

I explain that when the breathing rate increases, we usually take in more air, which can make the throat feel different. I guide clients to recognize that during heightened anxiety, their throat may feel like it is closing, or that they may stop breathing, although this has never actually happened. Similar to clients concerned about their heart, I sometimes recommend that these clients have a health check. This can help reduce fears they have regarding issues with their breathing.

Clients who experience acute anxiety episodes often worry that they may collapse. I explain that during extreme episodes of anxiety, it is normal to feel light-headed. I describe how this sensation is related to changes in their breathing. I usually encourage clients to consider that, although it may feel like they are about to collapse, how many times have they actually collapsed? Clients may believe they were close to collapsing many times, however, upon reflection, they realize they have never truly collapsed. If clients can remind themselves of this when they feel like they may collapse, it will assist them and reduce their anxiety levels.

For clients experiencing any of the feelings and thoughts described above, I usually also check their actions during acute anxiety episodes. Due to the sensations they encounter, clients often choose to sit, lie down, or lean on something for support. I explain that if they do this, they are sending their body a message through these actions, that they are not well, and this is likely to increase their anxiety.

Just as they need to challenge the thoughts they normally have when feeling very anxious, they also need to challenge their behaviors.

I usually check to see if clients carry out any other actions when feeling very anxious, such as standing in a "brace" position or pacing. Clients often develop patterns of behavior to try to cope with the acute anxiety they experience. However, these behaviors typically exacerbate the symptoms. I work with clients to establish alternative behaviors that will assist in decreasing the feelings of anxiety.

For example, it usually works best if clients can stand up when they feel very anxious, without bracing or leaning on anything, as this demonstrates that they are physically stable and will not collapse. Clients may feel like they are going to collapse; however, when they handle acute anxiety this way, they begin to believe that they will not collapse.

Square breathing

Another trick for managing anxiety

A further effective technique for managing anxiety is called "square breathing." This strategy may assist people experiencing either an acute anxiety episode or mild anxiety. I usually recommend this technique to all my clients who face anxiety-related concerns. I explain that this exercise involves counting slowly in their mind from one to three or four, depending on what feels most comfortable. The counting is combined with their breathing.

The steps are as follows:

1. First, they take a slow breath in, counting slowly in their mind from one to three or four as they inhale.

2. Next, they hold their breath for another count of one to three or four.

3. Then, they breathe out slowly, counting again as they exhale.

4. Finally, they hold the breath out for the same count before beginning the cycle again.

If they can continue this for a few minutes, it can rapidly ease anxious sensations and promote a sense of calm.

I describe this breathing technique as being in the shape of a square, with each of the four steps representing a side of the square. This visualization helps clients remember the steps. I also explain that it does not matter where they start with the square breathing; they can begin with any of the four steps described above. I usually encourage clients to practice this exercise when they are not feeling anxious, as this makes it easier for them to carry out when anxiety does occur.

Square breathing is essentially a distraction technique. While clients focus on where they are in the "square" and on the number they are counting to, their attention is drawn away from the anxiety. Furthermore, as they breathe in a slow steady rhythm, their breathing slows naturally, which in turn reduces anxiety. I also explain to clients that square breathing is a private exercise and not something to inform anyone about while they are completing it.

Clients also need to remain in the situation where they are experiencing anxiety and continue with whatever they are doing while completing the square breathing. By staying in the situation, this sends a message to the body that they are safe, which further assists in reducing their anxiety.

You may not experience episodes of anxiety where you feel you need this technique; however, it can be a useful strategy if you ever find yourself in a stressful situation. A woman informed me that she found the square breathing technique beneficial during childbirth, as it helped her calm down. I have also used this strategy myself on a few occasions when asked at short notice to speak in front of large groups, and I can personally vouch for its effectiveness.

Cardiovascular exercise

An essential component in overcoming anxiety

I explain to clients that undertaking regular cardiovascular exercise can help desensitize them to feelings of mild anxiety and increase their ability to cope. Clients with anxiety may have avoided exercise for some time; therefore, I recommend they consult their physician to ensure it is safe for them to begin an exercise program.

Following their health check, I encourage clients to gradually increase their exercise. I explain that they could start with a brisk walk, then progress to a jog, and gradually increase the intensity. I emphasize that it is important for them to increase the distance of their walk or run each time, as this will also boost their confidence.

When clients with anxiety first attempt cardiovascular exercise, they often slow down as soon as they notice their heart rate and breathing rate increase, because it feels uncomfortable. I explain that stopping the exercise as soon as it feels uncomfortable will not help them overcome the anxiety.

I encourage clients to continue the exercise for at least a few more minutes after they begin to feel uncomfortable, as this will help desensitize them to the sensations they feel and boost their confidence.

Increase your resilience to anxiety

During therapy with clients who experience anxiety issues, I also take time to explain factors that may increase their anxiety. Being aware of these factors helps clients understand the reasons behind elevated anxiety levels. The main factor that can increase anxiety is fatigue. When people feel tired, their general confidence usually decreases, negatively affecting their thinking and reducing their tolerance to feelings of anxiety.

Other factors that may increase anxiety are related to different physical aspects, such as being in pain, feeling hungry, being dehydrated, or being too hot or cold. The more clients are affected by these factors, the more likely their anxiety levels will increase, or they will be more prone to experiencing anxiety. Therefore, I explain to clients that one of the best ways to increase their resilience to anxiety is by caring for themselves physically, ensuring adequate rest, nutrition, and hydration.

Stimulants

Is your diet affecting your mental health?

It is beneficial to address factors that could be changed to help reduce a client's anxiety levels in conjunction with therapy. Therefore, I usually spend time educating clients about foods and drinks that contain caffeine, as caffeine has been found to be related to increased levels of anxiety (Winston, et al., 2005). For example, I explain that caffeine is not only present in coffee, it is also found in energy drinks, tea, and chocolate.

I then explain to clients how these items may be increasing their anxiety levels and suggest they consider reducing certain foods and beverages from their diet. I usually recommend that they try removing energy drinks, for example — which contain a substantial amount of caffeine and other stimulants — from their diet for a week to see if they notice any changes in their anxiety levels.

I also encourage clients to become aware of how they feel directly after consuming specific products. This can help them identify if there are any items in their regular diet that could be removed to significantly reduce their anxiety levels. When clients try this approach, they are often surprised by how something like a piece of cake or a particular snack food can affect their mood.

I have noticed that clients often experience significant reductions in anxiety when they reduce caffeine or additives, especially artificial colorants, from their diet. Furthermore, incorporating calming additions such as chamomile tea, and replacing sugary or caffeinated drinks with water to maintain hydration, may also help reduce anxiety."

It can be an interesting experiment to become aware of how you feel after consuming certain products and to observe if there is anything you regularly eat or drink that may be increasing your overall levels of anxiety.

Exposure Therapy

Exposing clients to what they fear most

Are there any situations you avoid?

Strategies to overcome this

The other essential part of managing anxiety involves a form of exposure therapy, where clients are encouraged to gradually increase their exposure to situations that make them feel anxious. People with anxiety often avoid specific situations to escape those feelings, which may provide short-term relief. However, avoiding these situations typically leads to increased anxiety over the long term.

If clients can gradually increase exposure to a situation that makes them feel anxious, their confidence in these situations will usually slowly improve. The method of gradually increasing exposure to anxiety-provoking situations not only helps reduce anxiety in that specific situation, it also has a broader impact. The anxiety reduction tends to generalize to other environments, boosting a client's confidence in many areas.

A situation that often causes significant anxiety for clients I work with is being out in public. Many clients have limited the number of places they will visit. In extreme cases, some clients rarely leave the house without someone accompanying them, restricting outings to necessary visits, such as to a doctor.

Going to the supermarket is commonly an anxiety-provoking situation, and I use exposure therapy to address this. Clients with extreme anxiety might always go to the same supermarket and only with someone else. I encourage them to start spending time alone in the supermarket and to gradually increase this time.

As a first step, this may involve leaving the person they usually accompany for only a few minutes while walking down a different aisle on their own. I encourage them to gradually spend more time alone in the supermarket until they are able to cope with completing the shopping independently. It is essential for clients to build their confidence gradually, with each step of exposure. For example, in exposure to the shopping environment, they might spend only a few minutes alone in the store, several times before they can extend this duration.

With increasing exposure to stressful situations, it is more effective to focus on one factor at a time. For example, a client might only visit the supermarket very early in the morning to avoid crowds. The factors to address with this example, therefore, are the time of day, the length of time in the environment, and being alone in the store.

I focus on each area and encourage clients to gradually increase exposure, such as choosing different days and times to visit the store. Once a client becomes comfortable, for example, with visiting the store at a different time, I then encourage them to address another aspect of the situation, continuing to build their comfort and confidence.

I explain the importance of meeting the targets that clients set. For example, if clients set a goal of spending "five minutes alone in the store," it is vital that they achieve this goal. I have worked with several clients for whom shopping has been challenging and highly anxiety-provoking, and they have often felt the need to leave their shopping trolley behind and rush out of the store.

I explain to clients that leaving in such a manner sends a message to their body through their behavior, that they are not safe in that environment. This action will perpetuate the anxiety surrounding that situation. I advise clients that the next time they are in an environment where they feel anxious and want to leave, they need to look at their watch and decide to stay for a set time before leaving. Ideally, this would be for the five minutes set as the goal, however in some cases, even staying an additional twenty seconds is an achievement and will assist them.

The key is that the client has taken control of the situation and determined when they will leave, even if it is only for a short while. This increases the client's confidence and makes it more likely they will stay even longer next time. When I can identify a specific place where a client feels anxious about going and work on this, their confidence usually increases in various locations.

I often work with clients who have experienced specific traumas, and they feel anxiety when exposed to something that reminds them of these events. For example, I work with many clients who have been involved in motor vehicle accidents.

These clients often completely avoid the area where the accident occurred or may even stop driving altogether, as it creates too much anxiety. I work with these clients to gradually increase exposure to factors associated with the accident, such as driving closer to the location where it occurred.

Often, other factors need to be addressed, such as when clients avoid driving at night because the accident took place during that time. I address this issue by encouraging clients to begin with longer drives around sunset, followed by short drives after dark, gradually increasing both the duration and their comfort with night driving.

If clients have stopped driving altogether, a first step may be for them to sit in their vehicle at home for several minutes each day, gradually increasing this time. A second step could involve encouraging them to drive only a short distance on roads near their home, gradually extending their driving time and distance. A final step would be to encourage them to drive to the location where the accident occurred.

If you can identify places you tend to avoid or spend less time in because they make you feel anxious, these strategies may be beneficial. Your comfort zone is likely much broader, and your ability to tolerate challenging situations greater than that of many clients I have worked with. However, recognizing situations where you feel anxious and gradually increasing your exposure to them can improve your confidence. For example, speaking to large audiences is a situation that often triggers anxiety for many people. Gradually increasing audience size and exposure can help desensitize this response.

Exploring thoughts further

Strategies to encourage behavior change: Targeting social anxiety

When working with clients diagnosed with anxiety, I also focus on addressing their thought processes. As mentioned previously, specific thoughts can intensify the symptoms during an acute anxiety episode. To help reduce a client's anxiety in certain situations, particular lines of inquiry can assist the client in viewing things from different perspectives. The first area I explore involves asking clients to consider what the "worst-case" scenario might be if they entered a situation they have been avoiding.

For instance, if a client is apprehensive about attending a party due to social anxiety, I would ask them what they perceive as, "the worst that could happen," if they attended. Often, clients harbor fears about situations they have not thoroughly explored. In the context of a party, clients frequently express concerns about feeling embarrassed or ignored. In our sessions, I explore with them what the worst aspect of experiencing these feelings might be. While acknowledging that such feelings would be uncomfortable, I encourage clients to consider that they would be safe and manage to cope with the situation. Often, clients have developed quite extreme or dramatic worry over a situation. I assist them to view the situation more realistically, encouraging them to recognize that they will, in fact, survive it.

Other clients with social anxiety often worry that others will be able to see their anxiety. I explain to these clients that there is a common misperception about how visible anxiety is to others. In reality, it is often difficult for others to identify anxiety. I also ask clients to try to recall the last time they were able to notice someone else looked anxious or embarrassed. Typically, clients struggle to remember a time when they could clearly identify someone else's anxiety.

Another common fear among clients with social anxiety is the concern that their face will redden when they feel anxious, and that others will notice. When clients express this worry, I ask them when they last noticed someone with a red face. Most find it difficult to recall such a time. However, if they do recall seeing someone with red cheeks, they usually acknowledge they assumed the person was simply warm. I then explain that even if someone did notice the redness in their face, others would likely think the same — that they were just feeling hot.

Clients with social anxiety often exhibit negatively biased thinking about being around others, such as assuming they will not enjoy themselves in social settings. I address this mindset by encouraging clients to explore alternative perspectives. In these situations, I encourage them to consider that they might even enjoy themselves. I typically ask if they know anyone who will be present and whether they have previously enjoyed the company of that person.

If a client can remember a time when they socialized with this person and enjoyed themselves, it reinforces the idea that they might enjoy the experience again. By changing how clients think about these situations, they are encouraged to attend social gatherings they might have previously avoided.

Additionally, when discussing these scenarios with a client, they will usually visualize the situation as we talk about it. If they remember a previous time when they enjoyed the company of their friend and recall how they acted and felt during that time, it can assist them in recreating the same positive experience in the future. Through these visualizations, clients can increase their confidence in social situations and improve their behavior. This approach parallels basic sports psychology, where an athlete visualizes themselves performing well and scoring goals repeatedly, thereby enhancing their performance.

Exploring irrational fears

I also make it a point to discuss any fears the client may have about being in social situations. It is essential to thoroughly explore all fears with the client. A common concern among clients with social anxiety is the fear of being "trapped" in a situation for too long, which often deters them from attending. I collaborate with clients to develop strategies that allow them to leave an uncomfortable situation when necessary.

I explain to clients that it is important to have an appropriate way to exit a situation, such as saying they have a headache, even if the underlying reason is anxiety. They also need a preplanned method for leaving, such as having their own transportation or money for a taxi. As discussed earlier, I emphasize that it is crucial not to leave a situation the moment they start feeling anxious. Staying even a few minutes longer and reminding themselves that they are safe, and will manage to cope with the situation, can significantly boost their confidence and prove more beneficial in the long run.

Furthermore, people with social anxiety may find being around others for an extended length of time to be exhausting. Therefore, it can be helpful for them to know how long they will be in a particular situation. For example, planning to stay at a party for two hours, from 6:00 pm to 8:00 pm, can make the situation more manageable. If a client is enjoying themselves by 8:00 pm, they always have the option to extend their stay. However, having a set time limit provides structure and can make the situation more comfortable.

This strategy of setting a time limit on social situations may also encourage clients to go out. For instance, if clients are expected to attend a social function that might last several hours, they can decide beforehand to attend for just one hour, allowing themselves to leave following this time, if they feel overwhelmed. I recommend that this plan is something they keep to themselves or perhaps share with their partner. Often, if clients can motivate themselves to attend for this short time, they may find that once they are there, they are happy to stay longer.

I also explain to clients that the more details they know prior to attending, the less stressful the situation is likely to be for them. For example, knowing how many people will be at an event or what time dinner will be served can be very helpful. By being informed about as many details as possible in advance, clients can feel more in control of the situation, which can significantly reduce anxiety.

I encourage clients with social anxiety to gradually increase their exposure to social situations. This process might start by attending smaller gatherings with familiar people, and over time, progressing to larger functions as their confidence grows. It is also important for them to broaden the range of places they visit and to participate in events with different people and at various venues as part of their personal growth.

I have applied many of these strategies myself over time to boost my confidence when attending unfamiliar venues. One phrase I find particularly helpful is, "I will just have a look," when considering whether to attend an event. This aligns with the strategy of setting a time limit on participation, for example, saying, "I will attend for just one hour." An effective first step can be simply telling yourself, "Just have a look."

I have used this approach to attend large conferences, concerts and festivals alone. Once there, I tell myself, "I will just stay an hour and see how I feel." Usually, after that point, I become more comfortable and end up staying for the entire event. Reflecting on how often I have used this strategy, I realize that I have always managed to stay and enjoy myself. I highly recommend trying this for any event you would like to attend, even if it feels outside your comfort zone.

Confidence tricks: How your body language affects confidence

I dedicate time to helping clients with social anxiety understand the impact of body language and posture in managing anxiety. When people are anxious, they often hunch their shoulders instead of standing or sitting up straight. I emphasize the importance of being mindful of their posture and correcting it when they notice slouching. By adopting the posture typically associated with comfort and confidence, clients begin to feel more like this.

I educate clients with anxiety about the importance of maintaining appropriate eye contact. Through therapy, I encourage them to hold eye contact in public, even if it feels uncomfortable at first. By gradually increasing the length of time they can look people in the eyes when feeling anxious, clients will, over time, begin to feel more confident, and maintaining eye contact will become more comfortable for them.

I also spend time explaining to clients how people unconsciously mirror others' behavior and how they can use this understanding to their advantage. I inform clients that if they feel anxious, they might appear "unhappy," causing others to respond to this behavior, which can lead to uncomfortable social interactions. Additionally, I advise clients not to disclose their anxiety to others, as this can make the other person uncomfortable and potentially exacerbate the client's anxiety.

Therefore, I encourage clients, when attending social events, to "act" as they would if they felt confident and were enjoying themselves. By behaving as if they feel a certain way, their actions will reflect this confidence. Others are likely to respond positively to the confident or happy demeanor they project, leading to more positive interactions. This response, in turn, boosts their confidence. The longer a person can "act happy," or as if they are having a good time, the more they will genuinely start to feel this way. Eventually, this act can transform into their natural behavior.

It might be interesting to observe your behavior around others and experiment with this strategy. This can be a particularly useful trick if you find yourself needing to attend a social event when you are feeling tired or unenthusiastic about going. By applying this strategy, you will likely enjoy the event more than if you were to attend while outwardly displaying exactly how you truly feel about being there.

I believe everyone is acting a little, all the time, so I do not view this as being "fake." Instead, I see it as a basic strategy to enhance enjoyment for yourself and others. I have certainly used this approach myself and found it to be quite beneficial. Additionally, it is important to be mindful of whether you are smiling slightly when people speak to you and to appear interested, even if you are not. This also contributes to more positive social interactions.

Another strategy I discuss with clients who experience anxiety in public, is to redirect their focus to external factors. Clients with anxiety often have heightened awareness of their physiological state and any anxious sensations. I recommend that when they begin to notice these feelings, they first acknowledge to themselves that they feel anxious and that this is okay, then consciously focus their attention elsewhere. Dwelling on the bodily sensations of anxiety or fixating on internal dialogue about feeling anxious tends to escalate the anxiety.

I explain to these clients that they need to keep their focus on what they are doing and on external factors. Ideally, in a social setting, engaging in a conversation with someone can serve as an effective distraction. I emphasize that staying distracted can help reduce their anxiety. If the current topic is not engaging, I suggest they introduce a subject they find interesting. This increased interest in the conversation makes them less likely to ruminate on internal thoughts and feelings. In turn, this can assist in reducing the anxiety. By avoiding concentrating on their anxiety, they allow it to naturally begin to subside.

How understanding human memory can assist reduce anxiety

A final area I discuss with clients experiencing anxiety involves understanding how the human brain processes memory. Clients with anxiety often worry that others are observing them and judging them. I reassure the clients that noticing others is normal human behavior. It is a part of our basic programming and survival instincts, which historically helped us recognize potential threats and find mates. This instinct persists today. Consequently, I explain that when they are in public, it is natural for people to glance at them and then look away. I also encourage clients to observe that they exhibit the same behavior.

I then explain that it is also normal human behavior to make quick "judgments" about things, including people we see. As humans, one of the ways we make sense of the world is through classifying things and making judgments. Here are some brief statements that may run through someone's thoughts: "That person is tall," "That person is driving fast," or "I like that person's dress." When we make comments to ourselves about other people, it is not usually a statement about their personality. I explain to clients that we all have a constant dialogue running through our mind, and clients realize that they also have this continual internal dialogue.

Once a client understands this, I then explain some aspects of how human memory functions. I describe that our "working memory" and "short-term memory," which are closely related, only hold a certain amount of information. These areas of memory are responsible for processing what a person is currently doing and for temporarily storing information. If the information is considered important, it will then be stored in long-term memory. Minor day-to-day matters, such as what we ate for breakfast last week or whom we saw at the shops yesterday, are usually not relevant or essential to know in the long term and, therefore, are not retained.

To highlight this point, I usually ask clients to recall the last time they were at the supermarket. I help the clients realize that during this time, they would have noticed people at the store and perhaps made a brief comment about a person to themselves. I then ask the clients if they can remember the exact details of any one person's face from when they were at the store.

A client may have a vague memory of seeing someone there, although usually, he or she is not able to picture the person's face clearly. I explain that this is because such information is neither useful nor important to remember, and therefore, the brain does not retain it. The only exception to this example would be if a person lived in a small town where they were familiar with the people who worked at the store, and therefore, might remember one of the workers' faces.

The example is intended to highlight that, although people may make comments to themselves about someone they see in public, no information is retained about these individuals. I also point out to the client that, while someone may have noticed them at the shop and made a mental comment about them, that person will not be sitting at home thinking about the client.

I ask clients to reflect on how often they have noticed a stranger at the shops and made a brief internal comment about them, and how frequently they have found themselves thinking about that person later that day or in the following days. Clients quickly realize this is not something they do, and it is unlikely that others would do this either.

I explain to clients that just as they have many important things happening in their lives to focus on, so do other people. This is not something to be offended by; it is simply how people function. Individuals need to free up space in their working and short-term memory to focus on significant matters in their lives and what they are currently doing, rather than contemplating people they do not know. When clients with anxiety understand this, they usually feel more confident being outdoors, and it worries them less when people glance at them. It may be interesting to observe how this phenomenon plays out in your life. People's confidence generally improves when they realize that strangers are not really that interested in them.

This is something I remind myself of when I am out in public and my confidence is a little low due to tiredness or other factors. When people glance your way, it can be helpful to offer a small smile, which is often reciprocated.

I have worked with hundreds of clients who experience anxiety. From the most recent statistics I am aware of, anxiety is unfortunately on the rise. It is important to remember that many of the people you see out and about may also be having a difficult time, and feeling anxious too.

Anger Management

Release your anger in healthy ways: Effective ways to manage anger

During my time as a psychologist, I have observed clients struggling with allowing themselves to feel anger. I usually spend time explaining to clients that anger is a normal and healthy human emotion and can be useful. For example, if someone were to attack them, feeling angry would be advantageous, as it can be protective and energizing. Anger enables a person to either defend themselves or flee as necessary.

It is important for clients to understand that anger is not always a negative emotion. Most clients I have worked with spend a great deal of time trying not to be angry. I explain to them that it is not healthy to suppress any human emotion. Many clients tend to suppress anger, allowing it to build up over time. When this happens, people often express anger that is disproportionate to the situation. As a result, the accumulated anger is released in response to something insignificant. I work with clients to explain healthy ways they can release anger as needed.

Factors that affect anger levels

I explain to clients that there are self-care factors that are highly likely to impact a person's ability to manage anger. Foremost among these is regular exercise, which is vital for reducing stress and tension (Fleshner, 2005). Exercise stimulates chemicals in the brain that help individuals feel psychologically well (Dishman & O'Connor, 2009).

Other critical factors in managing anger include adequate nutrition and hydration. When someone feels hungry or dehydrated, they are more likely to experience anger in certain situations. Additionally, being overheated can also increase the likelihood of feeling angry. Moreover, it is important for a person to get sufficient sleep and relaxation time to effectively manage their anger levels.

A final factor that affects anger levels is physical pain. When someone is experiencing untreated pain, their general tolerance tends to be lower, making them more prone to feelings of anger. The better people care for their physical health and well-being, the easier it becomes for them to manage situations that might otherwise provoke anger.

Identify and minimize triggers

I work with clients to help them identify specific factors that trigger their anger. Recognizing these triggers and making changes to mitigate them can be highly beneficial. I recommend that clients modify as many anger-contributing factors in their environment as possible. For example, if a client notices they consistently feel angry when running late for appointments, they could adjust their routine by aiming to arrive thirty minutes early.

There may be simple changes a client can make in their home environment — for instance, if a client frequently bangs their knee on a particular table, moving the table can help. Although this sounds simple, there are often several factors a person can adjust that may be contributing to their anger levels. Another example is if a client has technological devices that cause frustration due to being unreliable or inefficient, upgrading these devices may eliminate them as triggers for anger.

It may be interesting to notice if there are any specific factors that make you feel angry and whether these can be removed or modified. While some factors in your environment may not be changeable, the more triggers you can identify and adjust, the less anger you are likely to feel.

How to manage anger experienced in the moment

I often provide clients with examples of healthy ways to release their anger. The first step is recognizing when they feel angry. Many people I have worked with in therapy have become so accustomed to suppressing their anger that they struggle to identify the emotion. This can be related to various factors, such as upbringing, as well as societal and cultural expectations. These clients were never encouraged to express emotions, especially the often negatively perceived emotion of anger.

Therefore, I encourage clients to start noticing when they feel angry. I advise them to rate their anger on a scale from 0 to 10 throughout the day, with "0" representing "no anger" and "10" representing "very angry." I recommend that they pause several times during the day to observe and rate their level of anger.

Once clients can recognize the initial stages of feeling angry, the next step is to label the emotion. I explain to clients that this simply involves saying to themselves, "I feel angry." I emphasize that noticing and labeling the emotion requires acceptance of the feeling, without any judgment. I encourage clients to practice this exercise, highlighting that it is purely about recognizing how they feel and the intensity of the feeling. The feeling itself is to be observed neutrally, not judged as negative or positive. It simply is what they are experiencing at that moment.

The second step I explain to clients is to try to locate where they feel the anger in their body. This helps them notice and observe the feeling, rather than suppressing it. After identifying where in the body they experience the emotion, without judging it, I recommend they tell themselves a statement in a neutral manner, such as, "I feel anger in my stomach."

A final step involves imagining what color and shape the anger might take. For example, a person might say, "I feel anger in my stomach; it feels like a tight red ball, and that is okay." The tone they use can even be a little sarcastic or humorous, which often helps.

Although we are focusing on the emotion of anger, this technique of identifying the emotion, locating where it feels most intense in the body, and associating it with a shape and color, can be an effective strategy to help a person identify and begin to release any emotion.

The main point I highlight with clients in this process is the importance of recognizing and acknowledging the feeling of anger as they experience it, instead of trying to suppress it. Once these steps are completed, the next phase involves releasing the anger in a healthy manner.

Anger typically involves a significant surge of energy in the body that needs to be released safely. Hitting something soft, such as a pillow or a bed, can be helpful. I explain to clients that releasing the emotion verbally can also be important. Screaming into a pillow or expressing the emotion in a private space, such as a forest, can be an effective way to release the anger from their body. I also advise that if the anger is only mild, clenching the fists and making a growling sound can provide enough release.

I emphasize to clients that these strategies need to be completed in private. It is therefore crucial for them to recognize their anger as quickly as possible. This awareness allows them to remove themselves from a situation and then release the emotion effectively.

I recommend that clients, when noticing anger arise while with someone, communicate with a statement such as, "I need a few minutes alone," and then move to a different room. This allows them to step away, release the anger, and then return to the interaction. I explain that shouting at someone only worsens matters. I encourage clients to recognize that it is far more beneficial to release anger privately and then return to the discussion in a calm and appropriate manner

Everyone experiences anger from time to time. Practice recognizing when you feel angry, and experiment with some of the strategies outlined above to release it. Those who are able to release anger as it arises tend to maintain better psychological health and feel less stressed, compared to those who routinely suppress their anger.

Managing anger toward a past event

Do you hold any anger toward a person or past event?

An effective strategy to release this anger

I have encountered clients who exhibit a low level of constant anger. In such cases, there is often someone or an incident from the past they feel angry about. I always assess whether they blame themselves or someone else for this. If they hold themselves responsible, I address it as mentioned in the chapter, "Challenging Beliefs Around the Past." If the anger and blame are directed toward a specific person, this is managed differently as described here.

In this circumstance, I recommend clients write an "anger letter." This is an effective strategy for releasing anger felt toward someone for a past event. This strategy is also effective in assisting the client to release anger felt toward a deceased person. Once we have identified who the client feels angry with, I encourage them to accept the emotion without feeling guilty about their feelings. This acceptance is the first step in effectively releasing the emotion.

I then recommend that the client write a letter to the person they feel angry with, expressing their feelings toward the person and the events that occurred. I emphasize that this exercise needs to be completed in private and the client is not to show this letter to anyone else. Knowing that this letter remains completely private allows the person to express themselves without censoring any feelings. I also recommend that the letter be handwritten.

The actual process of writing the letter by hand, rather than texting or typing, can be therapeutic in itself. While the letter can be typed or composed as a text message, handwriting is preferable. If clients choose to type the first draft of an anger letter, I advise using a blank document that can be easily deleted, or an email draft without entering an email address. If they prefer to write it as a text message, it needs to be created in a new message that is not addressed to anyone. This precaution helps prevent the message from being accidentally sent.

It is important that this letter is directed specifically to the person the client feels angry toward, and that sentences begin with "You...". Additionally, it is crucial that the letter does not include any form of self-blame. All blame and anger need to be directed toward the person they are angry with.

I explain to clients that the letter needs to include everything they feel angry about regarding a person's treatment of them. Full sentences are not necessary. I recommend clients use swear words as this can assist them to tap into their feelings of anger. The letter can be as short or as long as needed, and it is complete when the client feels they have expressed everything they truly want to say to the person.

Depending on the circumstances, it may be beneficial for the client to send a later draft of this letter to the person involved. This is a personal decision the client makes. The initial letter often needs to be rewritten, sometimes multiple times, and over several days. I typically recommend that a client re-read their first draft only once and then destroy it. Repeatedly reading this first draft can be upsetting and is generally not beneficial.

The final draft of the anger letter will usually contain clear sentences describing what the client experienced and how it made them feel. I usually recommend that, once clients believe they have completed the final draft, they leave it for a few days. When they revisit the letter later, they may choose to edit certain parts. It is vital that the client feels satisfied that the final draft includes everything they want to express.

Furthermore, the final draft ideally would not contain any anger or swear words and would be more of a statement of the client's experience. The letter is intended to educate the person about how they made the client feel in the past. This can be beneficial for the client, as knowing that the other person understands their past experiences can fulfill the psychological need for their feelings to be recognized. The most important component of this exercise is that the client feels they have had the opportunity to fully express themselves.

In face-to-face interactions, it can often be challenging to fully express ourselves, as certain aspects may be forgotten, or the other person may not listen respectfully. To release anger completely, clients need to feel that they have expressed themselves in their entirety. The power of a written letter is that the recipient cannot easily ignore it and may read it multiple times, unlike a text or email, which can be quickly deleted. Occasionally, clients might receive a response back from the person they have written to, although this is uncommon. However, obtaining a response is not the goal of this exercise.

The most important aspect is that the client feels they have been heard. It can be just as effective to address a letter simply to the person's first name, such as "Bob," without including an actual address. The client understands that the letter will never reach the specific person, yet the emotions are released through the process of writing and "sending" it.

Whether to post the letter depends on the individual circumstances of the client. In the case of a deceased person, the client might choose to place the letter on the person's grave. This is a personal decision. Another option is to send an anonymous letter, again depending on the specific situation. It is essential that all earlier drafts of anger letters be destroyed.

I explain to clients that it is normal for emotions such as sadness to surface while completing this exercise. This can be part of the process of releasing old hurt and anger. I encourage clients to complete this exercise by reassuring them that they will typically feel better once these emotions are released.

Frequently, clients express a preference to avoid thinking about past events because it upsets them. However, I explain that if they have never released this emotional pain, it can remain beneath the surface and have an impact on their overall psychological health. Many clients have shared that they felt better after completing this exercise. Some choose to bring in their anger letters to show me, although this is not necessary.

I explain to clients that this strategy can also be effective for releasing anger they may feel toward people currently in their lives. For example, if they are upset with their partner for something they have done, it can be helpful to write an anger letter directed to the person, describing exactly how they feel. I then recommend that they destroy this letter. I explain to clients that completing this exercise before discussing the matter with their partner helps, as the "raw" emotion of anger has been released. As a result, clients often find they can approach the discussion with their partner more calmly.

I also recommend to clients that writing an anger letter can help release anger they may feel toward certain people or situations where, expressing their anger directly would not be advisable. For example, they might feel angry toward their employer or a family member. It can be effective for clients to write a private anger letter directed to this person and then destroy the letter. When clients next see the person, they often find they do not feel as angry, as a significant portion of the anger has been released.

For example, I have worked with several clients who felt very angry toward their elderly mother or father, and there were valid reasons for this anger. However, it was decided that giving the letter to their parent would likely cause upset, might not resolve any issues, and could even create more problems. In these cases, it proved more beneficial to destroy all copies of the letters. Every situation is unique and needs to be considered based on individual circumstances.

If there is an incident from your past that causes you to feel angry toward someone, writing an anger letter can be a helpful exercise to release these emotions. A common indicator of anger is repeatedly replaying a past scenario in your mind involving this person, or frequently imagining what you would like to say to them. This suggests that there may be unresolved anger toward them that could be beneficial to address. It can be helpful to express these feelings in a private anger letter, as described above.

It may be useful to consider whether there are any people in your life, or situations involving others, perhaps from the past, toward whom you still feel anger. Writing a private anger letter, as described above, directed toward these individuals, can help release these feelings. The more anger is released in appropriate ways, the more psychologically healthy you are likely to feel.

This is a strategy I regularly use. I find it helpful to act as soon as I notice feelings of frustration or anger toward someone. This could even include frustration directed at a company or situations where support staff have not been able to assist me effectively. Typing a quick note expressing my frustration clearly and addressing it to "dear manager" or "support staff," I have found to be very helpful. I type this out swiftly, then delete it, take a few deep breaths, and usually revisit the situation later. This method allows me to release the raw feelings of frustration, enabling me to later send a rational and appropriate email that clearly states what I would like to be addressed.

Not taking on someone else's anger

Case example: "The angry man"

The strategies described above assist people in releasing anger from current or past situations. Unfortunately, many individuals are unaware of these strategies and carry a significant amount of unresolved anger that has accumulated over time. Through my work, I have often observed clients who have been upset by someone else's anger. It is important to remember that if someone is angry, it is their anger and usually their issue.

There may have been a minor trigger for an outburst, however, typically, the person was already angry before encountering you that day. This was illustrated to me one day as I waited for a train at London King's Cross station, one of the busiest train stations in London. The following story uses fictitious names and is based on what I observed that morning and what might have been occurring in, "Jim's" life.

Jim had a terrible morning. Nothing went right for him from the moment he awoke. He had overslept, with much to accomplish that morning. His partner was supposed to wake him earlier; however she had forgotten, a recurring issue that had exhausted his patience. He had contemplated leaving her for years. All they seemed to do was argue, and he could not remember the last time he felt happy in their relationship. Missing his train to work had meant that he missed an important meeting.

Anticipating stern words from his boss upon arrival, as he had been late on several occasions recently, added to his stress. Jim was not sleeping well and found concentrating at work increasingly difficult. His dissatisfaction with his sales job was growing, and he was far from meeting his monthly budget goals. This financial pressure, combined with the missed bonus, increased his stress as he worried about being on the verge of getting fired, having missed his targets for several months now.

It was a particularly hot day, and Jim had just boarded the late train, a service he disliked due to its usual overcrowding. This morning was no different; he did not even manage to find a seat, and the air conditioning was out of order. He was also hungry, having had no time for breakfast. Upon arriving at London King's Cross, Jim decided he needed some food before catching the connecting train to work. Since he was already late, he figured it did not matter much. The thought even crossed his mind to skip work entirely, as he dreaded facing his arrogant boss.

The events of the morning and the anger Jim felt about his life replayed continuously in his mind. Unbeknownst to him, this was evident in the angry expression etched on his face and the tense way he held his body, with fists clenched as he walked. He had spotted his unsuspecting target: a young 16-year-old working in the bakery named "Mandy."

As soon as Jim approached the counter, he noticed that none of his favorite pies were left; this was all the excuse he needed to unleash the anger that had been brewing within him all morning. "Why are there no pies left here?" he screamed at young Mandy. The teenage bakery assistant did her best to apologize, explaining that they had experienced an unusually busy morning and assuring him that a new batch of pies would be ready soon. However, Jim was uninterested in her explanation and continued shouting at her in front of the other customers.

Mandy began to shake from the stress, and eventually, tears started to flow. Seeing her cry, a smile appeared on Jim's face — he felt he had won this battle. Although Jim might not be "winning" at home or work, and despite his life being in disarray, he relished this small victory. He was satisfied. He had not really needed the pie; it was merely an excuse to vent his frustrations at someone. Mandy had no insight into Jim's personal struggles. Perhaps if she did, she might not have taken his tirade to heart and could have found the strength to stand up to him.

The way Jim appeared that morning and Mandy's reaction, were exactly as they happened. While Jim may not have had those specific issues in his life, there were likely reasons behind his anger. The intensity of his emotion was visible in his facial expression and posture. When people hold onto anger and allow it to build up, it often ends up being released onto someone else.

Typically, the individual is unaware of how much anger they have built up and does not consciously direct it at others. However, it is still, of course, inappropriate to vent one's anger at others, regardless of awareness. If someone is ever very angry at you, it is beneficial for your psychological well-being to remind yourself that it is their anger, not yours. Try to avoid taking it personally and, if possible, distance yourself from the person.

A key indicator for me in recognizing when I might be misdirecting anger, is noticing when something bothers me more than it usually would. If I find myself being less patient than normal, I reflect on whether anything earlier in the day has caused me frustration. If I can identify a factor that has contributed to my stress, I implement strategies outlined above, such as sending a brief email or using a physical tactic like clenching a towel while acknowledging my anger. I also consider biological factors discussed in previous chapters that may be influencing my mood. My aim is to address and release the anger swiftly and appropriately. I will also apologize if I have been somewhat short with someone.

Are You Sleeping Well? Tricks to Help You Sleep

Sleep trick number one: Sleep hygiene

How to use your environment to help you sleep

When I meet a client for the first time, I usually ask about their sleep quality. Sleep patterns provide valuable insight into an individual's psychological health. Poor sleep often correlates with increased depression. Fatigue can impact all areas of cognitive functioning, including memory and concentration.

I inquire whether clients are having trouble falling asleep or experiencing frequent nightmares. While occasional nightmares are normal, recurrent nightmares related to past experiences may require therapy. I also ask clients whether they frequently wake during the night, as waking with particular images on their mind can indicate unresolved issues that may benefit from therapeutic attention. Additionally, I compare their current sleep duration to their usual sleep pattern, as individuals experiencing depression often sleep longer than usual.

A predominant issue I have observed in therapy is difficulty falling asleep. Addressing this concern is often a priority in treatment, as improved sleep typically leads to better mental health. Once a client's sleep improves, other issues can be more effectively addressed.

An effective strategy I explain to clients to help them fall asleep more quickly is called, "sleep hygiene," which essentially means cultivating good sleep habits. This strategy is based on an information sheet developed by the Centre for Clinical Interventions (www.cci.health.wa.gov.au).

If clients are having trouble falling asleep, they often stay in bed for hours trying to get to sleep. This leads to an association that the bed is a place where time is spent thinking for hours before they sleep, and the person will become accustomed to this. Over time, this can make them feel more alert upon getting into bed. Part of sleep hygiene education involves teaching clients how to break this pattern.

I advise clients that if they are not asleep within approximately twenty minutes, they need to get out of bed and move to a different room. They then need to sit in this different environment and engage in a task that is not too stimulating for the mind, such as reading a simple magazine. I also recommend avoiding television and using electronic devices during this time, as these can be stimulating for the mind and usually keep a person awake.

I recommend keeping the room dimly lit, as bright lights can also stimulate the mind. Clients are advised to remain in the alternative environment until they feel sleepy, then return to bed and attempt to sleep. As before, if they are not asleep within approximately twenty minutes, they need to get up again and return to the other room, following the same instructions. They need to repeat this pattern as many times as required until they eventually fall asleep. Over time, clients therefore develop a new association: the bed becomes a place where they fall asleep within twenty minutes, rather than a place for prolonged thinking.

It is also important to avoid caffeine and sugar for a few hours before trying to fall asleep. I know a few people who are very sensitive to caffeine and will not consume coffee past mid-afternoon, as they find it interferes with their sleep. If you drink coffee, you could vary the timing of your last cup and observe when it is best for you to cease caffeine for the day.

It is also recommended that individuals use the bed exclusively for sleeping during this time of routine change. For instance, they need to avoid watching television or using electronic devices in bed, ensuring the bed is associated solely with sleep. Typically, altering this routine leads to improved sleep. However, there are exceptions where clients have pre-existing associations that aid sleep, such as reading or listening to calming music. If a client has consistently used such activities in the past to help them sleep, I suggest they continue these habits while also applying the twenty-minute rule after they stop reading or listening to music.

The final component of the sleep hygiene strategy involves addressing daytime fatigue. If clients feel tired during the day, a short sleep is acceptable, provided it lasts less than one hour and is taken before 3:00 pm. I recommend setting an alarm to ensure they do not sleep for longer than one hour during the day. By implementing this sleep hygiene strategy, clients typically fall asleep more quickly, which often leads to improved mental health. If you are experiencing difficulty falling asleep, sleep hygiene is a technique you can try on your own.

I also recommend that clients remind themselves while in bed that even if they are not asleep, they are still physically resting by lying in bed, which is beneficial. This mindset helps relieve the "pressure" of trying to fall asleep and promotes relaxation, which can aid sleep onset. Additionally, two other strategies that may help clients fall asleep more easily are relaxation techniques and a "body scanning" technique.

Sleep trick number two: A relaxation technique

A method to help relax your body and fall asleep more quickly

In this relaxation technique, a client learns to focus on specific body areas and understand how to relax their body. I instruct clients to gradually shift their awareness from one area of the body to the next, slowly. They can start either at the top of the head and move slowly downwards or begin at the toes and move their awareness slowly upwards through the body. From my experience, starting with awareness at the toes and progressing upwards tends to be more effective in helping people fall asleep.

During therapy, I guide clients on where to focus their attention, which can be very relaxing for them. I explain how to concentrate on one area at a time and how to move slowly up the body. Once they learn this technique, clients can practice it themselves at home while lying in bed, helping them to fall asleep.

I recommend clients start by focusing on the tips of their little toes on both feet, aiming to make this area feel as relaxed as possible. Once they are satisfied with the relaxation in this area, they need to slowly move their awareness up each little toe. The next step involves relaxing the adjacent toes on both feet, continuing this process across all the toes. After ensuring all the toes are completely relaxed, they need to gradually move their awareness up their feet. When they reach around the ankle areas, clients can shift their attention to their little fingers on both hands, beginning the relaxation process in these areas.

Clients begin by moving their awareness to the next finger on both hands and continue this process with each subsequent finger. While focusing on their fingers, it is important to regularly check back on their toes to ensure they remain relaxed. They then gradually guide their awareness along their arms and legs toward the center of their body. As they practice this technique, it is essential to focus on the sensation of each body area in contact with the bed while breathing deeply. Visualizing these areas "sinking" into the bed can further enhance relaxation.

I explain to clients that as they focus on different body areas, they will still be aware of their stream of conscious thoughts. I recommend not focusing on any particular thought and encourage clients to allow the thoughts to pass through their mind, without analysis. If they find themselves focused on their thoughts, I advise gently bringing their awareness back to their body and recalling where they reached in the relaxation process.

If you are having a difficult night falling asleep and have completed this strategy, and reaching the center of the body, simply begin again from the fingers and toes. It is important not to be mentally "hard" on yourself, as everyone experiences difficulty falling asleep from time to time. Maintaining a kind internal dialogue is crucial, including when you try a strategy and do not achieve the desired outcome as quickly as hoped.

Sleep trick number three: Body scanning

A distraction and muscle relaxation technique

A variation of the relaxation strategy described above is the "body scanning" technique, which can also help clients fall asleep more easily. I instruct clients to begin by lying comfortably in bed and affirming to themselves that they will be asleep by the time they count to ten. They then count slowly from one to ten, aiming that by the time they reach ten, their body will achieve the same state of relaxation as it would when they are asleep.

The client begins by counting "one" in their mind, then slowly scans their body to identify the area that feels the most tense. Once located, they focus their attention on that area, aiming to relax it so that it matches the level of relaxation felt elsewhere in the body. After they are satisfied that the area is as relaxed as the rest of their body, they can mentally say "two." I also explain to clients the importance of continually reminding themselves of their goal: to be asleep by the time they reach "ten," and to ensure their body achieves the desired level of relaxation by that stage.

I describe to clients the importance of imagining the "steps" from "one" to "ten" as being of equal increments. Clients are advised to only say "two" when they feel sufficiently relaxed at this second step, gradually moving toward their goal of being asleep by "ten." Between each number, they need to scan their body again to identify the next area of tension. They then focus on relaxing this area so it matches the relaxed state of the rest of the body. It is important for clients to ensure that their body is sufficiently relaxed before progressing to the next number, keeping in mind the goal of being asleep by the time they reach "ten."

I explain to clients that they will continue to have their conscious stream of thoughts while they are completing this strategy, and to remember that this is normal. As described above, I reiterate not to pay these thoughts any attention and to keep bringing their awareness back to their body. I emphasize to clients that if they find they are becoming focused on their thoughts, they need to remind themselves of the number they were on and bring their attention back to relaxing their body. If clients try this technique and are not asleep by the time they reach "ten," I advise them to go back to "one" and start again. However, if they go through the steps slowly enough, they are usually asleep before they reach "ten."

I suggest that if you have trouble falling asleep, you use the sleep hygiene technique in combination with either the relaxation technique or the body scanning strategy. Over time, you will work out a variation that suits you best, allowing you to utilize it whenever you have difficulty sleeping. Even if you can fall asleep easily, these relaxation techniques may help you fall asleep more quickly. Additionally, learning one of the sleeping strategies described above can be useful, providing you with a method to manage any future sleep difficulties as needed.

How to Change Behaviors and Habits

Is there a habit in your life you would like to change?

Changing habits the easy way

I often help clients with changing behaviors. This could be a habit they want to change themselves, or something that others, like an agency or a family member, have encouraged them to consider changing. The same methods can work well in either situation.

The first step in therapy is to help clients think differently about their behavior. Using a simple technique, they are encouraged to change their mindset about the habit, making it more likely that they will want to change the behavior. I support clients to make that decision for themselves and take steps toward changing the habit.

This powerful therapy technique involves helping clients identify all possible positive and negative consequences of a behavior and explores the potential implications of changing the habit. The same approach is used for various behaviors, whether it is reducing or stopping alcohol, drugs, or smoking, or beginning a healthy eating or exercise program. In this therapy, it makes no difference if a client wants to begin or cease a behavior; the same technique can be effective.

This strategy encourages behavior change by exploring possible consequences, rather than simply stating something is "negative" and in need of change. When people are told "not to" do something, they frequently resist. Therefore, discussing the behavior change openly and non-judgmentally with the client, is often more effective.

For instance, when working with a client who wants to cut down on drinking alcohol, we explore the potential consequences of changing or not changing this behavior during therapy. I have found it effective to write down everything the client mentions in two lists: one for the perceived positives or benefits of the behavior, and one for the negatives or possible consequences of the behavior. With alcohol use as an example, I begin by asking the client to list the "good things" they associate with drinking alcohol. Clients are often surprised by this approach, as they are accustomed to hearing only about the negatives.

With this technique, it is important to initially use a neutral inquiry approach, considering all possible positives and negatives without offering any opinions. The client is also encouraged to do the same. For instance, some clients may say that alcohol helps them "relax" or is their "only break from family duties." It is important for clients to reflect honestly on the perceived benefits of the behavior. This self-awareness can lead to valuable insights into why they continue certain habits.

During therapy, I encourage the client to also consider what the potential negative consequences of in this case, consuming alcohol, may be. For example, the client might say they are, "concerned about possible health issues," or they are "worried about the financial impact". I then ask the client to think about how things might look if they continue the behavior versus if they change it. With alcohol use, the client may consider that if they continue the same behavior, their family "might get upset, with them," or there might be "adverse effects on their health in the long term." I offer no judgment when the client is exploring these potentials during this part of the exercise.

I then encourage the client to consider how things might be different if they change their behavior and reduce the alcohol intake. Clients might say, for example, that they could, "feel healthier," or they may have "fewer arguments at home." During therapy we explore all possibilities and focus on the aspects most important to the client. All the client's statements are written down in the two lists.

Once we have covered everything the client can think of, I read both sides of the list back to them in a non-judgmental manner. Throughout this process, I emphasize that it is the client's decision how things might change in their life. This strategy usually increases a client's understanding of why they engage in certain behaviors, which typically encourages them to change these behaviors.

I also work with clients to apply this technique to their day-to-day choices in a non-judgmental manner. For instance, if they are trying to eat healthily and reduce sugary food in their diet, they can use the strategy outlined above to help them choose, for example, whether to eat a piece of cake. They can consider possible negative or positive consequences of eating the cake. For example, they might think, "I could have that piece of cake, although how would I feel afterward? I might feel sick from the sugar or need to exercise more tomorrow to burn off the calories. However, it is ultimately up to me." This is something to be considered and decided privately.

At the same time, it is also advisable to consider how it might look if they do not eat the cake, such as perhaps feeling better later and healthier overall. I encourage clients to remind themselves that it is their choice and that considering alternatives in a neutral, non-judgmental way is important. This approach is more effective than telling themselves they cannot eat the cake, which usually increases the likelihood that they will want to eat it. This alternate way of thinking can help clients make healthier and clearer decisions.

This is something you can try yourself. Notice your thoughts around any behaviors you wish to modify. Rather than saying to yourself you "have to" or "cannot" do something, try practicing the strategy above. You do not need to always write it down, although this can help. The important point is to consider the possible positives or negatives regarding this choice in a neutral manner. I have found this can assist in behavior change to a greater extent than telling yourself you are not do something.

Behavior by association

How understanding this can help you break a pattern

After addressing the thoughts regarding the behavior, I then work with clients to adjust their behaviors. One of the most important aspects I assist clients with is understanding that to change a behavior, they need to replace it. Using the alcohol example, I would explore with the client when and where they usually consume alcohol and discuss alternatives they could use.

For example, if the client usually drinks alcohol while watching television in the evening, we discuss what could replace this habit. If the client typically sits in the same chair, I also encourage them to break the pattern by choosing a different chair or room when watching television. The person then needs to have something they have decided on in advance to do, instead of drinking alcohol — such as having a cup of hot chocolate.

Most human behaviors are formed by associations. As in the above example, this person had formed the association between watching television in the evening and drinking alcohol. Therefore, this connection needs to be addressed and changed to assist the client reduce their alcohol intake. I would also explore whether there were other behaviors they regularly engaged in while drinking alcohol, such as having a particular snack. To support behavior change, it is beneficial to alter as many associations as possible, such as choosing a different snack or even temporarily avoiding watching television in the evening for a length of time, while the new habit is being established.

I may encourage a client to read a book, go for a walk, or have a bath in the evening instead, allowing these activities to become the new behavior. I usually suggest a replacement behavior based on what the client perceives as the "benefit" gained from the original behavior. For example, If the client perceives that the behavior was relaxing, I suggest other potentially relaxing activities. This enables the same need to be met by the new behavior. However, it is important that the client chooses what the replacement behavior will be.

How to further adapt your environment to help you change a behavior

The final area I focus on for clients who want to change their behavior involves assisting them in putting in "blocks" or "barriers" to reduce the behavior. For example, if a client wants to reduce their alcohol intake, I explore exactly what they are drinking and where it is stored in the house, (if they are drinking at home). Typically, clients have specific habits with their alcohol use involving what they consume and when.

For example, if someone drinks beer every evening and stores it in the fridge, I recommend that the beer be stored elsewhere. If they can make it more difficult to access the beer, such as storing it in a locked shed, rather than the fridge, the person is likely to consume less. Ideally, the person would not have any alcohol in the house at all, instead needing to go out and purchase it each time they decide to have a drink. This would make it much more difficult to access and would therefore help reduce consumption.

In order to change a behavior, it assists to replace it with an alternative behavior. For example, if a client is trying to reduce or cease drinking alcohol, I help them identify an alternative beverage, such as a low-sugar soft drink or cup of tea. It is generally more effective to choose a drink they would not typically consume and use this as a replacement for alcohol.

I explain to the client that as they are restricting access to the product they are trying to reduce, I encourage them to increase the availability of the replacement product. In this example, I recommend that the client leave the soft drink or tea on the kitchen counter where it remains visible and easily accessible, if it has been chosen as the replacement beverage. This will increase the likelihood that they will drink it.

This technique works with any behavior a client is trying to change. For example, if a client is attempting to eat more healthily, I recommend that they have healthy food prepared and ready in the fridge. If they need to keep any "unhealthy" foods in the kitchen for other family members, I suggest these be stored out of sight, such as at the back of a cupboard. I have worked with several people who wanted to increase their water intake. It proved effective to place bottles of water within easy reach, close to where they sat, both at work and at home. At the same time, beverages they were trying to avoid, such as high-sugar soft drinks, were stored away in cupboards.

There may be other environmental aspects that also need addressing, such as if the client regularly drives past a shop to purchase alcohol after work and buys certain drinks. In therapy, I explore if the person can drive another way home or go somewhere else, for example, to a different shop to buy a healthy snack food.

There may also be situations the client needs to avoid for a length of time to make the behavior change easier, such as avoiding people and places where they would normally drink alcohol. Usually, if this is the case, I will suggest that the person socializes somewhere else without alcohol and explains to their friends not drink alcohol around them at the present time.

Tricks to delay and reduce a behavior

It also assists clients to delay behaviors they are trying to change. For example, if clients are trying to reduce alcohol consumption and they usually drink every night when they arrive home from work at 6:00 pm, I would recommend they try to wait until 7:00 pm, and then 8:00 pm, before having a drink. I explain to clients that ideally, they could try to slowly delay the behavior until a later and later time. Furthermore, once it has reached the time they decided they would have a drink, they can also try to delay the behavior further, perhaps another thirty minutes.

Another way to delay a behavior, is for the client to say something to themselves such as, "I will have a drink after my shower" or "after my dinner," and delay the behavior this way rather than stating a specific time. Often, clients forget they decided they were going to have a drink after the activity and become distracted by other tasks, thus delaying the behavior even further. Distracting themselves with an alternative behavior creates a delay, and this can be another effective way to reduce and change the behavior.

A further strategy that assists clients is for them to make an agreement with themselves to change their behavior for a set length of time. For example, they may decide that they will not drink alcohol for one month. It is easier for a client to tell themselves that they will change their behavior for a certain length of time, rather than stating that they will "never" drink alcohol again. If a client sets the target of never consuming an alcoholic drink again, this extreme thinking and difficult goal may dissuade them from even trying.

If a more manageable goal is set, such as in this case, to consume no alcohol for a month, the client is far more likely to achieve it. When the client reaches the target, they can then set another goal of perhaps an additional month alcohol-free. If the behavior has been changed for several months, there is a high probability that this will become a permanent change. Usually, after a length of time such as this has elapsed, the client has developed alternative and replacement behaviors. As an alternative to setting a goal of changing the behavior for a certain length of time, it can also be useful to use an upcoming social event as the goal, such as deciding not to have an alcoholic drink until Christmas.

Gradual behavior change: One step at a time is easiest

I also explain to clients that it is usually easier to change behavior if this is done gradually. For example, if someone usually drinks four alcoholic drinks every night, they may reduce to three alcoholic beverages and a cup of tea, then to two alcoholic beverages and two cups of tea, and so on. The person may also reduce the number of days per week on which they drink alcohol. This usually makes the new behavior easier to adapt to as a person gradually replaces one behavior with another.

In specific instances, people may choose or need to change their behavior quickly and cease the behavior suddenly; this is usually more challenging for a person both physically and psychologically. If a person takes a certain amount of a substance on a daily basis and then ceases quickly, they may go into withdrawal and need extra support with this. It is important to consult with a healthcare professional when considering any significant behavior change, particularly if substances or withdrawal may be involved.

I usually encourage clients to make the behavior change gradually if this is an option. I also recommend to clients that it is preferable to address one behavior they wish to change at a time, as this may be easier for the body to tolerate.

To successfully change a behavior, the more of the above aspects that are addressed, the easier it is likely to be. If you have any behaviors in your life you would like to change, you could try using some of the ideas described above. Once you learn these strategies to encourage behavior change, you can apply them to any area of your life.

Motivation Tricks

How to break tasks down to make them more easily achievable

I regularly work with clients to assist them with motivation strategies. Clients often tell me they have difficulty motivating themselves, and there are strategies to help with this. Firstly, I explain to clients that if they can make a start with something, it will be easier to carry on the task. For instance, if they need to clean their house, they could commit to just ten minutes of cleaning. Usually, once they begin, even if only for a few minutes, they find it easier to continue after getting started.

Another example would be if a client wanted to go for a one-hour walk. Walking for an hour may seem overwhelming and a great deal of effort, which might dissuade them from going at all. However, if clients state they will walk for, "just ten minutes," it enables them to make a start. Once they are outside and complete the ten-minute walk, there is a strong likelihood they will continue their walk, and they may even complete the full hour.

The trick is encouraging people to make a start. This method is effective for any task a person needs to complete. For example, if someone has a large report to write, they can tell themselves to "make a start on it," or to spend "one hour writing." After working on it for an hour, they will likely feel inclined to continue. This approach is far more effective than initially aiming to complete the whole report, as this might seem overwhelming. If a task appears too large, people often delay starting it.

I also explain to clients that breaking the task down into smaller parts can make it appear more manageable. For example, if someone needs to pack all the items in their house because they are moving, it might seem overwhelming. However, breaking it down into smaller tasks, such as planning to pack one room per day, can make the overall task easier to accomplish. People also feel satisfaction when a task is completed. Therefore, setting the task of packing one room and completing it will be more motivating than setting the goal of packing the whole house. Achieving small goals on the way to a larger goal helps people feel motivated.

A task can also be broken down into smaller parts by setting a time-based goal. As in the example above, if someone needs to move house and feels overwhelmed by packing, they could set the intention to spend two hours packing boxes. After completing the two hours, they will likely feel a sense of achievement. They may then choose to continue for another two hours, and perhaps a further two hours. This way, the person will have packed for six hours in total — whereas, if this had been the initial goal, it might have seemed overwhelming, and they might not have started at all.

This technique is also beneficial for tasks that may feel too difficult because they involve work in an unfamiliar area. Tackling these tasks step by step, using the strategies mentioned above, can be highly effective as well. Even if the task feels intimidating at first, such as learning new software, breaking it down into smaller manageable actions can make it feel far less overwhelming. Progress may be gradual, however each small step builds confidence and momentum. With persistence and patience, tasks that may have felt daunting can be completed.

Positive reinforcement: Make this work for you

I also explain to clients that setting a positive reward for task completion is essential. People are often driven by positive rewards, even if they do not realize this is a motivating factor. A positive reward is when a person sets a task with the understanding that, upon completion, they will reward themselves. This approach helps individuals complete the task and makes it more likely they will repeat it in the future.

People often set small rewards for themselves, sometimes without being aware of it. For instance, a person may say to

themselves, "I will wash the dishes and then have a cup of tea."
In this example, the drink of tea serves as the positive reward.
Another example of positive reinforcement is receiving
payment for work.

I explain to clients that if they consciously set a positive
reward for themselves before completing a task, they are more
likely to complete the task. For example, they could decide that
they will relax and watch their favorite television show after
finishing their housework. This strategy can be effective for any
task they need to complete.

I explain to clients that setting small positive rewards, as
discussed above, can motivate them, and it is beneficial to set
larger positive rewards as well. For example, many people plan
enjoyable weekend activities after a week of work, which is a
form of positive reinforcement. Additionally, people typically
set larger rewards throughout the year, such as taking an annual
vacation after several months of work.

These motivation strategies can help you complete various
small or large tasks. I recommend becoming aware of the
positive reinforcements you already use throughout your day
and week and consider whether these need to be increased.
Experiment with the motivation strategies mentioned above to
see which ones work best for you in starting and completing
tasks.

I certainly use the above-mentioned motivation strategies as often as possible. If I notice I am procrastinating on a task, it is usually because I have forgotten to break it down into smaller steps. When I have large reports to complete or lengthy documents to read, I remind myself, "I will just take a look at it." Breaking tasks down into one-hour blocks has also been quite effective for me. I hope you find some of these motivational strategies useful as well.

Conclusion

I hope you have enjoyed learning about the psychology strategies and techniques discussed throughout this book. Different sections may feel more relevant to you presently in your life. Other sections may be more useful at later stages, depending on your circumstances.

It is my hope that you have gained new insights and practical tools to assist you with everyday challenges. I also hope this book has empowered you with strategies to support your well-being across different areas of your life.

There is often great value in speaking with a non-judgmental therapist in a counseling setting. However, the more independently you can draw on effective psychological strategies, the more equipped you will be to navigate life's challenges on your own.

I wish you all the very best on your self-care journey towards lasting psychological health. You might revisit any section of this book whenever you need a gentle reminder, a new idea, or supportive encouragement along the way.

References

Blumenthal, J. A., Michael A., Babyak A., et al. (2007). Exercise and pharmacotherapy in the treatment of major depressive disorder. *Psychosomatic Medicine, 69*(7), 587–596.

Centre for Clinical Interventions. *Postpone your worry.* https://www.cci.health.wa.gov.au/~/media/CCI/Mental-Health-Professionals/Generalised-Anxiety/Generalised-Anxiety---Information-Sheets/Generalised-Anxiety-Information-Sheet---05---Postpone-your-Worry.pdf

Centre for Clinical Interventions. *Sleep hygiene Information sheet.* https://www.cci.health.wa.gov.au/~/media/CCI/Mental-Health-Professionals/Sleep/Sleep---Information-Sheets/Sleep-Information-Sheet---04---Sleep-Hygiene.pdf

Dishman, R. K., & O'Connor P. J. (2009). Lessons in exercise neurobiology: the case of endorphins. Mental Health & Physical Activity, 2(1), 4–9.

Fleshner, M. (2005). Physical activity and stress resistance: Sympathetic nervous system adaptations prevent stress-induced immunosuppression. *Exercise & Sport Sciences Reviews, 33*(3), 120-126.

Moasheri, B. N., Sharifzadeh, G., Nahardan, M., & Soofi, K. (2016). The effects of music therapy on depression among students. *Modern Care Journal, 13*(1), 1-5.

Stewart, A. E., Roecklein, K. A., Tanner, S., & Kimlin, M. G. (2014). Possible contributions of skin pigmentation and vitamin D in a polyfactorial model of seasonal affective disorder. *Medical Hypotheses, 83*(5), 517- 525.

Winston, A. P., Hardwick, E., & Jaberi, N. (2005). Neuropsychiatric effects of caffeine. *Advances in Psychiatric Treatment, 11*(6), 432-439

About the Author

Rebecca has an extensive background in psychology and worked as a clinical psychologist for nineteen years. Rebecca holds a Bachelor of Arts (Psychology), a Bachelor of Psychology (Honors), and a Master of Psychology (Clinical). She is a member of the Golden Key International Honour Society, in recognition of her academic achievements, and received the Clinical Practice Award in her Master's graduating class.

During her psychology career, Rebecca completed assessment work for the Federal and Youth Court of South Australia. She also worked for the Department of Child Protection and the Education Department in South Australia. Rebecca spent seventeen years in private practice, focusing on adult mental health.

Rebecca currently works as a life and wellness coach. She has always been passionate about helping individuals reach their highest potential and successfully navigate psychological challenges. Her experience spans a wide range of mental health issues, and she finds great fulfillment in witnessing her clients' personal growth and achievements. Rebecca has contributed to various fields, having worked as a care worker in disability services and volunteered as a teacher in Nepal.

www.ingramcontent.com/pod-product-compliance
Lightning Source LLC
Chambersburg PA
CBHW072012090426
42740CB00011B/2167